Grade 2

W9-BCG-108

Treasures

Grammar

PRACTICE BOOK

Macmillan
McGraw-Hill

B

The McGraw·Hill Companies

Macmillan
McGraw-Hill

Published by Macmillan/McGraw-Hill, of McGraw-Hill Education, a division of The McGraw-Hill Companies, Inc., Two Penn Plaza, New York, New York 10121.

Copyright © by Macmillan/McGraw-Hill. All rights reserved. No part of this publication may be reproduced or distributed in any form or by any means, or stored in a database or retrieval system, without the prior written consent of The McGraw-Hill Companies, Inc., including, but not limited to, network storage or transmission, or broadcast for distance learning.

Printed in the United States of America

9 10 021 09 08

Contents

Unit 1 • Relationships

School Days
David's New Friends

Statements 1
Statements and Questions 2
Mechanics 3
Proofreading 4
Review and Assess 5

Making Friends
Mr. Putter & Tabby Pour the Tea

Commands 6
Exclamations 7
Mechanics 8
Proofreading 9
Review and Assess 10

Firefighters at Work
Time For Kids: "Fighting the Fire"

Subjects 11
Subjects 12
Mechanics 13
Proofreading 14
Review and Assess 15

Being Yourself
Meet Rosina

Predicates 16
Predicates 17
Mechanics 18
Proofreading 19
Review and Assess 20

Coming to America
My Name Is Yoon

Sentence Combining: Subjects 21
Sentence Combining: Predicates 22
Mechanics 23
Proofreading 24
Review and Assess 25

© Macmillan/McGraw-Hill

Unit 2 • Growth and Change

Plants Alive!
The Tiny Seed

Nouns 26
Nouns 27
Mechanics 28
Proofreading 29
Review and Assess 30

Animal Rescue
A Harbor Seal Pup Grows Up

Plural Nouns 31
Plural Nouns 32
Mechanics 33
Proofreading 34
Review and Assess 35

A Hospital Visit
Time For Kids: "A Trip to the Emergency Room"

Proper Nouns 36
Proper Nouns 37
Mechanics 38
Proofreading 39
Review and Assess 40

How Animals Grow
Farfallina and Marcel

Possessive Nouns 41
Possessive Nouns 42
Mechanics 43
Proofreading 44
Review and Assess 45

Staying Fit
There's Nothing Like Baseball

Review Plurals 46
Review Possessives 47
Mechanics 48
Proofreading 49
Review and Assess 50

© Macmillan/McGraw-Hill

Unit 3 • Better Together

Telling Stories
Head, Body, Legs, A Story from Liberia

Action Verbs 51
Action Verbs 52
Mechanics 53
Proofreading 54
Review and Assess 55

Safety First
Officer Buckle and Gloria

Present-Tense Verbs 56
Subject-Verb Agreement 57
Mechanics 58
Proofreading 59
Review and Assess 60

Creatures Old and Older
Time For Kids: "Meet the Super Croc"

Past-Tense Verbs 61
Past-Tense Verbs 62
Mechanics 63
Proofreading 64
Review and Assess 65

Curtain Up!
The Alvin Ailey Kids: Dancing As a Team

The Verb *Have* 66
Past Tense of *Have* 67
Mechanics 68
Proofreading 69
Review and Assess 70

On the Farm
Click, Clack, Moo: Cows That Type

Sentence Combining: Sentences 71
Sentence Combining: Predicates 72
Mechanics 73
Proofreading 74
Review and Assess 75

© Macmillan/McGraw-Hill

Unit 4 • Land, Sea, Sky

Animal Needs
Splish! Splash! Animal Baths

Linking Verbs 76
Linking Verbs 77
Mechanics 78
Proofreading 79
Review and Assess 80

Animal Survival
Goose's Story

Helping Verbs 81
Helping Verbs 82
Mechanics 83
Proofreading 84
Review and Assess 85

Helping Planet Earth
Time For Kids: "A Way to Help Planet Earth"

Irregular Verbs 86
Irregular Verbs 87
Mechanics 88
Proofreading 89
Review and Assess 90

Wild Weather
Super Storms

Irregular Verbs 91
Irregular Verbs 92
Mechanics 93
Proofreading 94
Review and Assess 95

Habitats and Homes
Nutik, the Wolf Pup

Contractions 96
Contractions 97
Mechanics 98
Proofreading 99
Review and Assess 100

© Macmillan/McGraw-Hill

Unit 5 • Discoveries

Life in the Desert
Dig, Wait, Listen: A Desert Toad's Tale

Pronouns 101
Plural Pronouns 102
Mechanics 103
Proofreading 104
Review and Assess 105

Play Time!
Pushing Up the Sky

Pronouns, *I* and *Me*, ... 106
Pronouns, *We* and *Us* 107
Mechanics 108
Proofreading 109
Review and Assess 110

Exploration
Time For Kids: "Columbus Explores New Lands"

Possessive Pronouns 111
Possessive Pronouns 112
Mechanics 113
Proofreading 114
Review and Assess 115

In the Garden
The Ugly Vegetables

Pronoun-Verb Agreement 116
Pronoun-Verb Agreement 117
Mechanics 118
Proofreading 119
Review and Assess 120

Our Moon
The Moon

Contractions 121
Contractions 122
Mechanics 123
Proofreading 124
Review and Assess 125

© Macmillan/McGraw-Hill

Unit 6 • Expressions

Count on a Celebration!
Mice and Beans

Adjectives 126
Adjectives 127
Mechanics 128
Proofreading 129
Review and Assess 130

Creating Stories
Stirring Up Memories

Use the Article *a* 131
Use the Article *an* 132
Mechanics 133
Proofreading 134
Review and Assess 135

Worlds of Art
Time For Kids: "Music of the Stone Age"

Adjectives that Compare 136
Adjectives that Compare 137
Mechanics 138
Proofreading 139
Review and Assess 140

Inventors Then and Now
African-American Inventors

Adverbs 141
Adverbs 142
Mechanics 143
Proofreading 144
Review and Assess 145

Other People, Other Places
Babu's Song

Synonyms 146
Antonyms 147
Mechanics 148
Proofreading 149
Review and Assess 150

© Macmillan/McGraw-Hill

Name _____

- A **sentence** is a group of words that tells a complete thought.
- Every sentence begins with a capital letter.
- A **statement** is a sentence that tells something. It ends with a period.

School is fun. We play in the gym.

Circle each sentence. Then complete each incomplete sentence. Write it on the lines below.

1. Our classroom is sunny.
2. Writes on the chalkboard.
3. We read books.
4. Like art class.
5. Recess is a fun part of the day.

_____

_____

_____

_____

© Macmillan/McGraw-Hill

At Home: Have your child draw a picture of school and write three complete sentences about it.

Name _____

- A **question** is a sentence that asks something. It ends with a question mark.
- A **statement** is a sentence that tells something. It ends with a period.
- Begin each statement and question with a capital letter.

Do you have a pencil? I have paper.

Read the sentences. Circle each question and underline each statement.

1. Do you have homework?
2. I have lots of homework.
3. What do you have to do?
4. I have to read a story.
5. The story is about a pig.
6. Does Frank have homework?
7. Frank has to write a story.
8. What kind of story will he write?
9. Will he write a funny story?
10. No, he will write a scary one.

© Macmillan/McGraw-Hill

At Home: Ask your child a question about school. Have him or her turn your question into a statement.

Name _____

- Begin each sentence with a capital letter.
- End a statement with a period.
- End a question with a question mark.

We have gym today.
What is in my backpack?

Read the sentences. Write the sentences correctly on the lines.

1. what do you bring to school

_____

2. i bring books and a pencil

_____

3. what else is in your backpack

_____

4. my lunch is in my backpack

_____

5. what did you bring for lunch

_____

6. do you want to sit with me at lunchtime

_____

7. my new teacher is nice

_____

8. Are we in the same class

_____

© Macmillan/McGraw-Hill

At Home: Have your child write one sentence describing a character from a favorite book. Then have him or her write a question to ask that character.

Name _____

- A sentence tells a complete thought.
- Begin each sentence with a capital letter.
- End a statement with a period.
- End a question with a question mark.

Read the passage. Circle each mistake in capitalization and punctuation. Then rewrite the passage correctly on the lines below.

Today is Monday What do we do first. the teacher Reads a story. then we have math. does each child have a pencil. Now we are ready to begin the lesson

_____

_____

_____

_____

© Macmillan/McGraw-Hill

At Home: Have your child write a question and a statement about school. Then have him or her proofread for mistakes.

Name _____

Add the correct end mark to each sentence.
Write S next to each statement.
Write Q next to each question.

1. Our new school opens today _____
2. The brick building has three floors _____
3. Where is your classroom _____
4. The playground has three swing sets _____
5. How tall is the shiny new slide _____
6. Did you see the new music room _____
7. There is a band concert tonight _____
8. My sister plays in the school band _____
9. What instrument does she play _____
10. Do you have tickets to the concert _____

© Macmillan/McGraw-Hill

At Home: Review this page together.

Name _____

- A **command** is a sentence that tells someone to do something. It ends with a period.

  Share with your friends. Listen to your mother.

Circle each command.

1. I like to play games.
2. Treat the animals with care.
3. Sing a song with me.
4. Where does your friend live?
5. Share your cookie.
6. My dogs are my best friends.
7. I am going to Laura's birthday party next week.
8. Sit next to me.
9. Who gave you that flower?
10. Take me to the park.

Write two new commands on the lines.

_____

_____

_____

_____

© Macmillan/McGraw-Hill

At Home: Ask your child to think of a dog and list four commands to teach the dog.

Name _____

- An **exclamation** is a sentence that shows strong feelings. It ends with an exclamation point.
- Begin each exclamation with a capital letter.

  We love the zoo!
  Wow, those are huge elephants!

Underline each exclamation.

1. Today is Saturday.
2. Hooray, we are going to the zoo!
3. We will see many animals.
4. That giraffe is gigantic!
5. The lions look hungry.
6. Oh no, I'm scared!
7. The seals are so cute!
8. What time do you feed the seals?
9. The zoo closes in one hour.
10. We had so much fun!

Write two new exclamations on the lines.

_____

_____

© Macmillan/McGraw-Hill

At Home: Ask your child to use exclamations to tell about something exciting that happened.

Name _____

- Begin each sentence with a capital letter.
- End each command with a period.
- End an exclamation with an exclamation point.

Help your friend. This homework is hard!

Read the sentences. Write the sentences correctly on the lines.

1. please come to my birthday party.

_____

2. this is an awesome party

_____

3. cut the cake now

_____

4. i'm stuffed

_____

5. turn the music down

_____

6. play cards with me

_____

7. this is fun

_____

8. please help me clean up

_____

© Macmillan/McGraw-Hill

At Home: Work with your child to find a command and an exclamation in a newspaper or magazine.

Name _____

- Begin each sentence with a capital letter.
- End a command with a period and an exclamation with an exclamation point.

Circle each capitalization and punctuation mistake. Then rewrite the passage correctly on the lines.

let's go to our baseball game. you are up to bat first Watch out, here comes the ball. hit it hard. hooray, it's a home run.

_____

_____

_____

_____

© Macmillan/McGraw-Hill

At Home: Have your child write a command and an exclamation and then proofread the sentences.

Name _____

Add a period to each command.
Add an exclamation point to each exclamation.

1. Hooray, the sun is shining brightly ____
2. Come and play in my yard ____
3. Look at our new puppy ____
4. Gosh, your puppy is so little ____
5. Roll over ____
6. Oh no, the puppy rolled in the mud ____

Add or take away words to rewrite the sentences.

7. Make this statement a command.

   Jake scratches the puppy's belly.

   _____

8. Make this statement an exclamation.

   Your puppy is cute.

   _____

© Macmillan/McGraw-Hill

At Home: Review this page together.

Name _____

- Every sentence has two parts.
- The **subject** tells who or what does something.

Firefighters put out a fire.
subject

Dogs like to run.
subject

Underline the subject in each sentence.

1. The man calls the fire station.
2. The family leaves the house.
3. Everyone looks at the flames.
4. A fire truck races to the house.
5. The firefighters are just in time.

Write another sentence about a fire. Circle the subject.

6. _____

_____

© Macmillan/McGraw-Hill

At Home: Have your child make up simple oral sentences and identify the subject in each one.

Name _____

- You can correct some incomplete sentences by adding a subject.
- A **subject** tells who or what does something in a sentence.

Incomplete sentence: live at the firehouse

Complete sentence with a subject: The firefighters live at the firehouse.

Add a subject to the incomplete sentences and rewrite them on the lines below.

1. Visited the firehouse.

_____

2. Climbed inside a red fire truck.

_____

3. Taught us about fire safety.

_____

4. Told us never to play with matches.

_____

5. Told us to write about fire safety for homework.

_____

_____

© Macmillan/McGraw-Hill

At Home: Ask your child to underline the subject added to each incomplete sentence.

Name _____

- Begin the greeting and closing in a letter with a capital letter.
- Use a comma after the greeting in a letter.
- Use a comma after the closing in a letter.

Dear Mom,

Love,

Kim

Rewrite the letter correctly.

dear Grandma and Grandpa

I am having a great time on vacation. I miss you.

love

Juan

_____

_____

_____

_____

_____

© Macmillan/McGraw-Hill

At Home: Have your child write you a letter that uses correct punctuation and capitalization.

Name _____

- Begin the greeting and closing of a letter with a capital letter.
- Use commas after the greeting and closing in a letter.

Rewrite the letter correctly on the lines below.

dear Mom and Dad

am having a great time at camp. sing around the campfire. takes good care of us. can't wait for visiting day!

love

Maria

_____

_____

_____

_____

© Macmillan/McGraw-Hill

At Home: Have your child write a letter to a friend. Have him or her underline the subject in each sentence and then proofread the letter.

Name _____

Write C next to each complete sentence and circle the subject. Write I next to each incomplete sentence. Then add a subject and rewrite the sentences on the lines below. Underline the subject.

1. Our family has a fire escape plan. ____
2. My mom drew a map of our house. ____
3. shows the way out of the house. ____
4. practiced the escape plan many times. ____
5. Our meeting place is on the corner of our street. ____

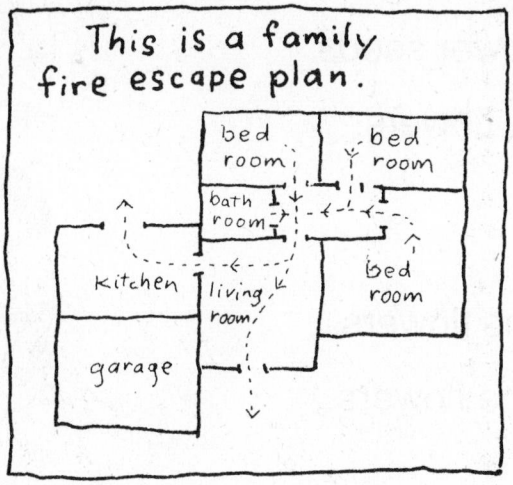

_____

_____

_____

_____

© Macmillan/McGraw-Hill

At Home: Review this page together.

Name _____

- There are two parts to every sentence.
- The **subject** tells who or what the sentence is about.
- A **predicate** tells what the subject does or is.

Jane plants flowers.
predicate

Which sentence tells about the picture? Draw a line under the predicate of that sentence.

1. **a.** Jane plants flower seeds.
   b. Jane picks the flowers.

2. **a.** Jane smells the flowers.
   b. Jane waters the flowers.

3. **a.** The flowers are pink and yellow.
   b. The sun shines on the flowers.

4. **a.** The flowers are dying now.
   b. Jane picks the flowers now.

© Macmillan/McGraw-Hill

At Home: Have your child write two new sentences about Jane and then underline the predicate in each sentence.

Name _____

- A **predicate** tells what the subject of a sentence does or is.
- You can correct some incomplete sentences by adding a predicate.

  Incomplete sentence: My dad

  Complete sentence: My dad loves vanilla ice cream.

Match each subject with a predicate to make a complete sentence. Then write the sentences on the lines below.

1. An ice cream truck	dropped his cone.
2. The driver	ate her cone quickly.
3. Mia	drove into the park.
4. Sam	sold ice cream.

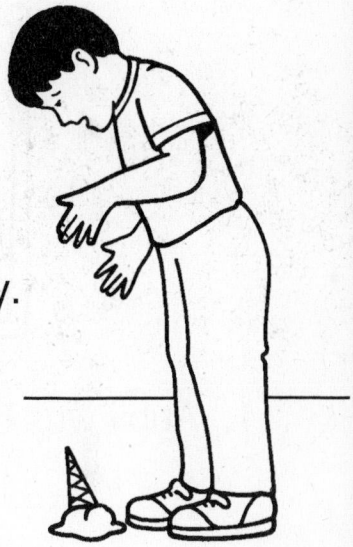

1. _____

2. _____

3. _____

4. _____

© Macmillan/McGraw-Hill

At Home: Write different subjects for four sentences. Have your child write four predicates to complete them.

Name _____

- Use a comma between the day and year in a date.
- Use a comma between the names of a city and a state.

August 17, 2006 Denver, Colorado

Read the sentences. Make the corrections. Write the correct sentences on the lines.

1. Abby was born on February 6 1998.

_____

2. She was born in Brooklyn New York.

_____

3. Her family moved to Portland Oregon.

_____

4. They moved on October 14 2003.

_____

© Macmillan/McGraw-Hill

At Home: Ask your child to write sentences that tell the city, state, date, and year he or she was born.

Name _____

- Use a comma between the day and year in a date.
- Use a comma between the names of a city and a state.

Draw a line below each mistake in the letter. Then rewrite the letter correctly on the lines.

Dear Uncle Ted,

I can't wait to visit you in Los Angeles California! We are coming on December 23 2007. I'll be sad when we leave there on January 2 2008.

It is so cold here in Burlington Vermont! The snow.

Love,

Noah

_____

_____

_____

_____

_____

_____

© Macmillan/McGraw-Hill

At Home: Have your child write a letter to a relative and then proofread the letter.

Name _____

Fill in the circle next to the predicate of the sentence.

1. My sister Rosa made a clay boat.
   - ○ My sister Rosa
   - ○ a clay boat
   - ○ made a clay boat
2. She entered the boat in an art contest.
   - ○ She entered
   - ○ entered the boat in an art contest
   - ○ boat in an art contest
3. The boat won first prize.
   - ○ won first prize
   - ○ The boat
   - ○ first prize
4. Rosa is taking art classes now.
   - ○ Rosa is
   - ○ art classes
   - ○ is taking art classes now
5. Her teacher called her a true artist.
   - ○ called her a true artist
   - ○ a true artist
   - ○ Her teacher

© Macmillan/McGraw-Hill

At Home: Review this page together.

Name _____

- If two sentences have the same predicate, you can combine them to make one sentence.
- You can combine sentences by joining two subjects with ***and***.

Ana learned English. Pedro learned English.

Ana and Pedro learned English.

Combine the subjects in each pair of sentences to make one sentence. Write the new sentence on the lines.

1. Ana moved here from Chile.
   Pedro moved here from Chile.
   _____

2. Our teacher welcomed Ana.
   The principal welcomed Ana.
   _____

3. Josh played soccer with Pedro.
   Hope played soccer with Pedro.
   _____

4. Ana made friends.
   Pedro made friends.
   _____

© Macmillan/McGraw-Hill

At Home: Have your child write pairs of sentences about his or her friends using the same predicates and then combine each pair using *and*.

Name _____

- If two sentences have subjects that are the same, you can combine the sentences.
- You can combine sentences by joining the predicates with ***and***.

Aki was born in Japan. Aki lives in America.

Aki was born in Japan and lives in America.

Combine the predicates in each pair of sentences to make one sentence. Write the new sentence on the line.

1. Aki speaks Japanese. Aki writes in English.

_____

2. Aki has brown hair. Aki is tall.

_____

3. Emily sat next to Aki. Emily shared her snack.

_____

4. Aki plays basketball. Aki jumps rope.

_____

© Macmillan/McGraw-Hill

At Home: Have your child suggest two short oral sentences with the same subject and then combine the two sentences.

Name _____

- Use **quotation marks** at the beginning and end of what a person says.
- A quotation shows the exact words that a person says.

"I like America," said Tamar.

Read each sentence. Write the corrected sentence on the lines.

1. This is Tamar, said our teacher.

_____

2. I moved here from Israel, Tamar said.

_____

3. Welcome to our school, Liz said.

_____

4. Thank you, said Tamar.

_____

5. The teacher asked, What kind of books do you like to read?

_____

_____

6. Tamar answered, I love to read books about dinosaurs.

_____

_____

© Macmillan/McGraw-Hill

At Home: Ask your child to write about a conversation and add quotation marks around the exact words spoken.

Name _____

- Sometimes you can combine sentences by joining two subjects or two predicates with ***and***.
- Use quotation marks at the beginning and end of what a person says.

Write the passage correctly on the lines. Add quotation marks where they are needed. Combine sentences that have the same subjects or predicates.

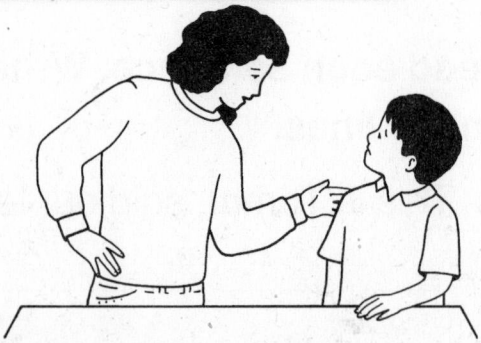

Miguel moved to Austin, Texas. His family moved to Austin, Texas. He starts his new school soon. He starts his new soccer team soon. Miguel is worried.

I miss my friends, Miguel said.

You will make new friends, said his mom.

_____

_____

_____

_____

_____

© Macmillan/McGraw-Hill

At Home: Have your child continue the story about Miguel.

Name _____

Combine the subjects or the predicates in each pair of sentences to make new sentences. Write the new sentences on the lines.

1. Nejal lived in Turkey.
   Her family lived in Turkey.
   _____

2. Her father got a job in Virginia.
   Her father moved the family here.
   _____
   _____

3. Nejal studied hard.
   Nejal learned English quickly.
   _____

4. I met Nejal first.
   I introduced her to all the kids.
   _____
   _____

5. She smiled at everyone.
   She made friends easily.
   _____
   _____

© Macmillan/McGraw-Hill

At Home: Review this page together.

Name _____

- A **noun** is a word that names a person, place, or thing.
- Some nouns name **people**.

A girl mows the lawn. Her dad plants a tree.

Circle the noun in each sentence that names a person.

1. Mom grows a vegetable garden.
2. Dad picks the vegetables.
3. My brothers eat the snap peas.
4. My sister likes the tomatoes.

Write two more sentences on the lines below. Include a noun that names a person in each one. Use the picture for ideas.

5. _____

_____

6. _____

_____

© Macmillan/McGraw-Hill

At Home: Ask your child to make up oral sentences with nouns and identify those nouns that name people.

Name _____

- A noun is a word that names a person, place, or thing.
- Some nouns name **places**.

  This is my backyard.

- Some nouns name **things.**

  The flowers are yellow.

Read the sentences. Underline the nouns that name things. Circle the nouns that name places.

1. Many plants grow in the forest.
2. We saw evergreens in the mountains.
3. You can see a cactus in the desert.
4. What trees grow in your town?

Write two more sentences on the lines below. In one sentence, include a noun that names a place. In the other sentence, include a noun that names a thing.

5. _____

_____

6. _____

_____

© Macmillan/McGraw-Hill

At Home: Have your child write a sentence to answer the question in item 4.

Name _____

- Use commas to separate three or more words in a series.
- The word ***and*** or ***or*** comes before the last word in a series.

I see flowers, plants, and trees.

A rose may be yellow, white, red, or pink.

Read each sentence. Write the corrected sentence on the line.

1. I need to buy pots soil and seeds.

_____

2. Do you want to plant tulips daisies or roses?

_____

3. Flowers need sun air and water to grow.

_____

4. Will you plant flowers in the front back or side yard?

_____

5. I will give flowers to my sister my aunt and my mom.

_____

Write another sentence about plants. Include three or more words in a series.

6. _____

_____

© Macmillan/McGraw-Hill

At Home: Have your child write a sentence that lists three favorite foods.

Name _____

- A noun is a word that names a person, place, or thing.
- Use commas to separate three or more words in a series.

Read the passage. Correct all the mistakes you find.

Cara Max and Jack hiked up a mountain. they saw trees insects and flowers along the way. For lunch they each had a sandwich a yogurt and a drink. At the end of the hike, Max said I'm tired!

Go back and circle each noun in the passage. Write all the nouns on the lines below.

_____ _____ _____

_____ _____ _____

_____ _____ _____

_____ _____ _____

_____ _____ _____

© Macmillan/McGraw-Hill

At Home: Have your child identify each noun from the passage as a person, place, or thing.

Name _____

Circle the nouns in each sentence.

1. My uncle opened a shop in the city.
2. People can buy fresh fruit and vegetables there.
3. My aunt grew those berries in her garden.
4. Farmers grow other foods in their fields.
5. A huge truck brings some corn.

Write the nouns that you circled in the correct column.

People	Places	Things
_____	_____	_____
_____	_____	_____
_____	_____	_____
_____	_____	_____
		_____
		_____

© Macmillan/McGraw-Hill

At Home: Review this page together.

Name _____

- A **singular noun** names one person, place, or thing.
- A **plural noun** names more than one person, place, or thing.
- Add ***-s*** to form the plural of most nouns.

I have one dog. Mia has two dogs.

Use the pictures to fill in each blank with a plural noun.

1. The bird is eating two _____.

2. Three _____ are sleeping.

3. The _____ are feeding the fish.

4. There are five _____ in the nest.

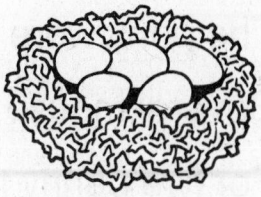

© Macmillan/McGraw-Hill

At Home: Have your child name things around the house that have more than one, such as chairs and books.

Name _____

- Add ***-es*** to form the plural of singular nouns that end in ***s, sh, ch,*** or ***x.***

  fox ⟶ foxes lunch ⟶ lunches

- To form the plural of nouns ending in a consonant and ***y,*** change ***y*** to ***i*** and add ***-es.***

  pony ⟶ ponies

- Some nouns change their spelling to name more than one.

  mouse ⟶ mice man ⟶ men

Read the sentences. Make the underlined nouns plural. Write them on the lines.

1. The school child took a trip to the farm. _____
2. How many bus did they fill up? _____
3. The pony were eating grass. _____
4. Several mouse were in the barn. _____
5. For five penny they could feed the animals. _____

© Macmillan/McGraw-Hill

At Home: Write singular nouns, and have your child write the plurals. Then switch tasks.

Name _____

- Begin the greeting and closing of a letter with a capital letter.
- Use a comma after the greeting in a letter.
- Use a comma after the closing in a letter.

Write the letter on the lines. Use capital letters and commas where they belong.

dear Aunt Yoon

Sam and I went to a fair today. Many other children were there. We rode on ponies. We had fun! We miss you.

love

Jing

_____

_____

_____

_____

_____

© Macmillan/McGraw-Hill

At Home: Have your child write about a recent trip. Help him or her check for correct use of commas and capitals.

Name _____

- Check the spelling of all plural nouns. Add ***-es*** to nouns that end in ***s, sh, ch,*** or ***x.***
- When you write a letter, check that the greeting and the closing begin with capital letters.
- Use commas after the greeting and closing in the letter.

Find each mistake in spelling of plural nouns, capitalization, and commas. Then rewrite the letter correctly on the lines below.

dear Ms. Green

Thank you for reading your storys to our class. We really liked the one about the three fox who live in three box. The story about the ponys who turned into mouses was great!

yours truly
Mr. Troy's Class

_____

_____

_____

_____

© Macmillan/McGraw-Hill

At Home: Have your child write the letter again using different plural nouns.

Name _____

Complete each sentence with the nouns in ( ).
Write the nouns in their plural form.

1. The tiny _____ needed help. (bird)
2. Their _____ had fallen from the _____. (nest, branch)
3. The _____ worked together to help. (child)
4. The _____ picked up some small _____. (girl, twig)
5. The _____ added _____ of cloth. (boy, scrap)

6. The baby _____ were hungry. (fox)
7. They ate _____ from the _____. (berry, bush)
8. Some _____ came to eat the _____. (mouse, seed)

© Macmillan/McGraw-Hill

At Home: Review this page together.

Name _____

- Some nouns name special persons, places, or things.
- This kind of noun is called a **proper noun**.
- A proper noun begins with a capital letter.

Carlos was born at Oakwood Hospital.

Circle the proper nouns.

1. Carlos lives in New Jersey.
2. He goes to Orchard School on King Street.
3. His teacher is Mr. Fleming.
4. At recess he plays tag with Al and Sara.
5. After school the friends play at Miller Park on Oak Street.
6. On rainy days, they play Monopoly.
7. Sometimes they go to Reed Library near Reed River.
8. They like to look at the pictures in *Science World Encyclopedia*.

© Macmillan/McGraw-Hill

At Home: Have your child write three sentences that include proper nouns.

Name _____

- Some proper nouns name days of the week, months, and holidays.
- The name of each day, month, or holiday begins with a capital letter.

Sunday June Father's Day

Choose the proper noun that names a day, month, or holiday. Write it correctly on the line below.

1. january
winter
vacation

_____

2. flag
vote
presidents' day

_____

3. holiday
flowers
mother's day

_____

4. sunday
day
afternoon

_____

5. fireworks
summer
july

_____

6. vacation
labor day
weekend

_____

7. september
school
teacher

_____

8. thanksgiving
fall
family

_____

© Macmillan/McGraw-Hill

At Home: Ask your child to write the names of holidays and the months in which they are celebrated.

Name _____

- An **abbreviation** is a short form of a word.
- An abbreviation begins with a capital letter and ends with a period.
- Most titles of people are abbreviations.

Mrs. Ms. Mr. Dr.

Find the mistakes. Write each sentence correctly on the line.

1. mr Jones broke his arm.

_____

2. mrs Jones drove mr Jones to the hospital.

_____

3. dr Jimenez took an x-ray of his arm.

_____

4. ms Rose, the nurse, helped the doctor.

_____

© Macmillan/McGraw-Hill

At Home: Have your child write sentences about his or her teachers and doctors using Ms., Mrs., Mr., and Dr.

Name _____

- The names of special people, places, or things begin with capital letters. The names of days of the week, months, and holidays begin with capital letters.
- An abbreviation begins with a capital letter and ends with a period.
- The greeting and the closing of a letter begin with capital letters. Use commas after the greeting and closing in the letter.

Find each mistake in capitalization and punctuation. Rewrite the letter correctly on the lines below.

dear dr moss

Thank you for seeing me on thursday. It was very nice of you to come to elwood hospital on thanksgiving. I hope you were still able to have a nice Holiday dinner.

yours truly

lisa

_____

_____

_____

_____

© Macmillan/McGraw-Hill

At Home: Have your child write a letter to a teacher, principal, doctor, dentist, or other adult.

Name _____

Circle the underlined words that are proper nouns.

1. Last Monday, our class went on a field trip.
2. Mr. Jones was our driver.
3. She drove from our school to Merrit Hospital.
4. Westside School is ten miles from the hospital.
5. The bus went through the Third Street Tunnel.
6. We met Maria Cortez and other nurses and doctors.
7. It was the month of February.
8. Valentine's Day was in two days.
9. Our teacher Ms. Adams had asked us to make cards for the sick children.
10. I gave my card to a girl named Josie.

© Macmillan/McGraw-Hill

At Home: Review this page together.

Name _____

- A **possessive noun** shows who or what owns or has something.
- Add an **apostrophe** (') and ***-s*** to a singular noun to make it possessive.

The dog's bowl is empty.

Choose the correct possessive noun. Write it on the line.

1. The _____ eyes are black.
   A. rabbit
   B. rabbit's

2. The _____ babies are called ducklings.
   A. ducks
   B. duck's

3. _____ kitten is orange.
   A. Maya's
   B. Maya

4. The _____ tail wags fast.
   A. puppy
   B. puppy's

5. The snake is _____ pet.
   A. Petes
   B. Pete's

© Macmillan/McGraw-Hill

At Home: Have your child use a possessive noun to write a sentence describing a family member's possessions.

Name _____

- Add an apostrophe to most plural nouns to make them possessive.

  The animals' barn is red.

- Add an apostrophe (') and ***-s*** to plural nouns that do not end in ***s***.

  The children's trip to the farm was fun.

Underline the correct plural possessive noun in ().
Rewrite the sentence on the line below.

1. I found several (birds'/bird's) nests in our yard.

_____

2. The (squirrel's/squirrels') tails are bushy.

_____

3. The (bear's/bears') bodies are very big.

_____

4. The (mice's/mices') noses twitch when they smell a cat.

_____

5. The (dog's/dogs') owners are training their pets.

_____

6. The (geeses'/geese's) beaks are wet.

_____

© Macmillan/McGraw-Hill

At Home: Help your child brainstorm a list of plurals and then make each plural noun possessive.

Name _____

- Always use an apostrophe to form a possessive.
- Add an apostrophe and ***-s*** to make a singular noun possessive.
- Add an apostrophe to make most plural nouns possessive.

Look at the picture. Then write the possessive of each noun on the line.

1. That _____ leash is on.

2. Both _____ tanks are open.

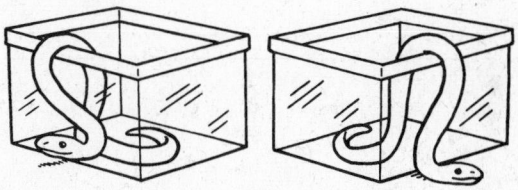

3. This _____ tail is curly.

4. The _____ bowls are on the floor.

5. The _____ bowl is on the table.

© Macmillan/McGraw-Hill

At Home: Have your child write phrases using both the singular and plural form of a noun.

Name _____

- Add an apostrophe and ***-s*** to make a singular noun possessive.
- Add an apostrophe to make most plural nouns possessive.

Circle each mistake. Rewrite the passage correctly on the lines below.

A frogs eggs are called egg spawn. The eggs shells protect the egg spawn. Soon the eggs hatch. Tadpoles come out. The new tadpoles tails are very long. Did you know that tadpoles eat frogs eggs?

_____

_____

_____

_____

_____

_____

© Macmillan/McGraw-Hill

At Home: Have your child describe an animal using possessive nouns.

Name _____

Mark the sentence that is rewritten correctly.
Underline the possessive noun in the correct sentence.

1. The wings of the butterfly are blue and black.
   - ○ The butterfly's wings are blue and black.
   - ○ The butterflies wings are blue and black.
   - ○ The butterflys' wings are blue and black.
2. The shells of the crabs are too small now.
   - ○ The crab's shells are too small now.
   - ○ The crabs shells are too small now.
   - ○ The crabs' shells are too small now.
3. The eggs of our duck are ready to hatch.
   - ○ Our ducks eggs are ready to hatch.
   - ○ Our duck's eggs are ready to hatch.
   - ○ Our ducks' eggs are ready to hatch.
4. The ears of the puppy are long and floppy.
   - ○ The puppies ears are long and floppy.
   - ○ The puppy's ears are long and floppy.
   - ○ The puppys' ears are long and floppy
5. The feathers of the swans have turned white.
   - ○ The swans' feathers have turned white.
   - ○ The swan's feathers have turned white.
   - ○ The swans feathers have turned white.

© Macmillan/McGraw-Hill

At Home: Review this page together.

Name _____

- A **plural noun** names more than one person, place, or thing.
- To change a singular noun to a plural noun, add ***-s*** or ***-es***. Do not add an apostrophe.

pool ⟶ pools box ⟶ boxes

Make the noun in ( ) plural. Then write the correct sentence on the line below.

1. The (player) are getting ready for the big game.

_____

2. Each team has ten (kid).

_____

3. How many (coach) are there?

_____

4. Ben threw four (pitch).

_____

5. Our team scored five (run).

_____

© Macmillan/McGraw-Hill

At Home: Lists items at a baseball game and have your child make each singular noun plural.

Name _____

- Add apostrophe (') and ***-s*** to a singular noun to make it possessive.

  The girl's towel is wet.

- Add an apostrophe to make most plural nouns possessive.

  Several swimmers' caps are white.

Circle the mistake in each sentence. Then write the possessive noun correctly on the line below.

1. The girls goggles are on their faces.

   _____

2. The boys suit is red.

   _____

3. The coachs whistle is around her neck.

   _____

4. All three swimmers laps are very strong.

   _____

5. The fans applause is loud.

   _____

© Macmillan/McGraw-Hill

At Home: Have your child use the possessive form to tell about something he or she is wearing.

Name _____

- Add an apostrophe and ***-s*** to make a singular noun possessive.
- Add an apostrophe to make most plural nouns possessive.
- Do not add an apostrophe to form a plural noun.

Underline the mistakes. Write the sentences correctly on the lines below.

1. Juans check-up is today.

_____

2. There are three doctor's at the office.

_____

3. Dr. Brown is a childrens doctor.

_____

4. The doctor listens to the boys' heart.

_____

5. Juan steps on Dr. Browns' scale to be weighed.

_____

6. Nurse Ann uses a chart to check Juan's eye's.

_____

© Macmillan/McGraw-Hill

At Home: Ask your child to use plurals and possessives to write two sentences about a visit to the doctor.

Name _____

- Add an apostrophe and ***-s*** to make a singular noun possessive.
- Add an apostrophe to make most plural nouns possessive.
- Do not add an apostrophe to form a plural noun.
- Use commas to separate three or more words in a series.

Find each mistake with plurals, possessives, and commas. Rewrite the passage correctly on the lines below.

At Ellas school, students choices for sports are tennis soccer and basketball. Ellas' mom and dad think she should play soccer. Her brothers favorite sport is basketball. Ella loves all sport's!

_____

_____

_____

_____

© Macmillan/McGraw-Hill

At Home: Have your child write a paragraph about a favorite sport and then proofread it.

Name _____

Circle the correct form of the noun to complete each sentence.

1. My coach showed us some special _____.
   stretch stretches stretchs
2. "Do these before all your _____," she said.
   practices practice practices'
3. Early in the year, we practiced in the _____ gym.
   schools schools' school's
4. Later in the spring, we used one of two soccer _____.
   fields' fields field's
5. My two best _____ moms are coaching this year.
   friends' friends friend's
6. They like to run _____ with us.
   lap's lappes laps
7. My _____ first game was a loss.
   teams teams' team's
8. Both _____ words after the game made us feel better.
   coaches' coach's coaches

© Macmillan/McGraw-Hill

At Home: Review this page together.

Name _____

- An **action verb** is a word that shows action.
- An action verb shows what someone or something is doing.

Isabel tells a story. Martin listens to Isabel.

Circle the action verb in each sentence. Write it on the line.

1. Justin sits in a chair. _____
2. He reads a story to his sister, Lucy. _____
3. Lucy listens to Justin. _____
4. She laughs at the funny parts. _____
5. Justin turns the pages. _____
6. He points to the pictures. _____

Write an action verb on the line to complete each sentence below. Use the picture to help you.

7. Justin _____ at his sister.
8. Lucy _____ Justin.

© Macmillan/McGraw-Hill

At Home: Have your child write one more sentence about Justin and Lucy that includes an action verb.

Name _____

- Some action verbs show actions you can see.

  Habib reads a book.

- Some action verbs tell about actions that are hard to see.

  Habib enjoys books about animals.

Read each sentence. Underline the action verb. Then write another sentence using that same verb.

1. The three bears walk in the woods.

   _____

2. Goldilocks likes the porridge.

   _____

3. Goldilocks sits in Baby Bear's chair.

   _____

4. She breaks the chair.

   _____

5. Goldilocks feels tired.

   _____

6. The bears come home.

   _____

7. The bears find Goldilocks asleep.

   _____

8. They chase Goldilocks away.

   _____

© Macmillan/McGraw-Hill

At Home: Have your child write sentences describing other things the three bears and Goldilocks do in this tale.

Name _____

- An **abbreviation** is a short form of a word.
- Most titles of people are abbreviations.
- An abbreviation begins with a capital letter and ends with a period.

Mister Fox
3 Forest Street
Portland, Oregon 97204

Mr. Fox
3 Forest St.
Portland, Oregon 97204

Draw lines to match the words in the left column with the abbreviations in the right column.

1. Mister	Ave.
2. Senior	Mr.
3. Doctor	St.
4. Avenue	Sr.
5. Captain	Dr.
6. Street	Jr.
7. Junior	Capt.

© Macmillan/McGraw-Hill

At Home: Have your child list all the abbreviations he or she knows.

Name _____

- An abbreviation is a short way of writing a word. It starts with a capital letter and ends with a period.
- Use an apostrophe and ***-s*** to make a singular noun possessive.

Read the paragraph and find the mistakes in abbreviations and possessive nouns. Rewrite the passage correctly on the lines below.

dr. Chen is a childrens doctor. He has lots of book's in the waiting room. mrs Gomez, the nurse, enjoys reading to the children when she has time. Poppleton is everyones' favorite story.

_____

_____

_____

_____

_____

© Macmillan/McGraw-Hill

At Home: Have your child write sentences about people. Ask him or her to include abbreviations in each sentence.

Name _____

Write the underlined word that is an action verb.

1. **Pedro makes** up great **stories**. _____
2. In one story, a **giant** ape **eats** a **huge** forest. _____
3. The ape **swallows whole** trees in **one** gulp. _____
4. Other **animals live** in the **trees**. _____
5. They **lose** their **homes because** of the ape. _____
6. So **they move** to the big **city**. _____
7. The animals **find new** homes in the city **parks**. _____
8. The giant **ape misses** the **other** animals. _____
9. **He plants** lots and lots of **new** trees. _____
10. **Soon** the animals **return** to the **forest**. _____

© Macmillan/McGraw-Hill

Name _____

- The tense of a verb tells when the action takes place.
- Present-tense verbs tell about actions that happen now.

Josh plays ice hockey.

His mom watches every game.

Draw a line under each present-tense verb. Then write the verb on the line.

1. Josh puts on his hockey skates. _____
2. He wears a helmet on his head. _____
3. Pads protect his knees. _____
4. Josh skates fast. _____
5. He hits the puck with a hockey stick. _____
6. Josh's mom cheers for him. _____

© Macmillan/McGraw-Hill

At Home: Have your child describe sports or activities and the equipment used.

Name _____

- A present-tense verb must agree with its subject.
- Add ***-s*** to most verbs if the subject is singular. Add ***-es*** to verbs that end with ***s, ch, sh, x,*** or ***z.***

  The car stops for the red light.

- Do not add ***-s*** or ***-es*** if the subject is plural.

  The children cross the street.

Draw a line under the correct present-tense verb in ( ). Then write another sentence using the same verb on the line below.

1. The woman (push, pushes) the swing gently.

   _____

2. The child (giggles, giggle).

   _____

3. The children (goes, go) down the slide one at a time.

   _____

4. Two boys (ride, rides) their bikes around the park.

   _____

5. One boy (wear, wears) a red helmet to stay safe.

   _____

6. The other (have, has) a green helmet on his head.

   _____

© Macmillan/McGraw-Hill

At Home: Have your child explain how he or she chose the verb in each sentence.

Name _____

- Use commas to separate three or more words in a series.
- Use ***and*** or ***or*** before the last word in a series.

  We play sports in summer, winter, spring, and fall.

Find the missing commas and rewrite each sentence correctly on the lines below.

1. We go skiing skating and sledding during the winter.

_____

_____

2. I ski slowly carefully and safely.

_____

_____

3. Do you like to ice skate roller skate or rollerblade?

_____

_____

4. I wear a helmet knee pads and elbow pads when I skate.

_____

_____

5. We can go sledding in my yard at the school or in the park.

_____

_____

© Macmillan/McGraw-Hill

At Home: Have your child write a sentence about three sports, using commas to separate the sports.

Name _____

- A present-tense verb must agree with its subject.
- Add ***-s*** or ***-es*** if the verb is singular.
- Use commas to separate three or more words in a series.

Find mistakes in the paragraph. Then rewrite the paragraph correctly on the lines below.

Each year a firefighter police officer or emergency worker come to our school. The firefighter teach us about stop drop and roll. The police officer tell us not to talks to strangers. We learns about 911 and giving our name number and address in an emergency.

_____

_____

_____

_____

_____

_____

© Macmillan/McGraw-Hill

At Home: Have your child write home safety rules and underline subject-verb agreement in each sentence.

Name _____

Write the present tense of the verb in ( ) to complete each sentence.

1. Rose _____ for the light to change. (watch)
2. Her little sisters _____ Mom's hands. (hold)
3. They all _____ both ways before crossing. (look)
4. Rose _____ about safety at school and at home. (learn)
5. The students in Rose's class _____ posters. (make)
6. Chan _____ a list of safety rules on his poster. (write)
7. One girl _____ a cartoon. (draw)
8. The cartoon _____ kids on skateboards. (show)
9. One skateboarder _____ too fast. (go)
10. The other skateboarders _____ safety rules. (follow)

© Macmillan/McGraw-Hill

At Home: Review this page together.

Name _____

- Verbs can tell about actions that already happened.
- These verbs are in the **past tense**.
- Add ***-ed*** to most verbs to tell about an action in the past.

  Our class learned about fossils last week.

  Our class looked at dinosaurs yesterday.

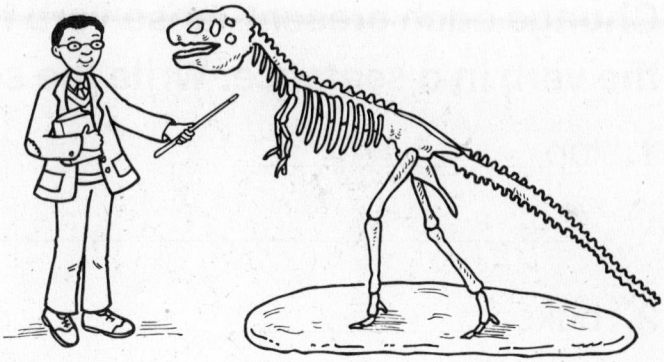

Circle the past-tense verb in each sentence. Write it on the line.

1. Our class visited the museum. _____
2. We learned about dinosaurs. _____
3. Did you know that dinosaurs once roamed the Earth?

   _____
4. I asked a question about Triceratops. _____
5. A scientist answered my question. _____

Choose one past-tense verb you circled above. Use it in a new sentence. Write the sentence on the lines.

6. _____

   _____

© Macmillan/McGraw-Hill

At Home: Have your child write sentences with other past-tense verbs.

Name _____

- If a verb ends with one consonant, double the consonant and add ***-ed***.

  The car stopped at the red light.

- If a verb ends with ***-e***, drop the ***e*** and add ***-ed.***

  The car moved at the green light.

Change each present-tense verb to past tense. Then use the verb in a sentence. Write the sentence on the line.

1. tap _____

   _____

2. bake _____

   _____

3. smile _____

   _____

4. trim _____

   _____

5. love _____

   _____

© Macmillan/McGraw-Hill

At Home: Say verbs in the present tense, and have your child say them in the past tense.

Name _____

- Begin the greeting and closing in a letter with a capital letter.
- Use a comma after the greeting of a letter.
- Use a comma after the closing of a letter.

Find the mistakes in the letter. Rewrite the letter correctly on the lines below.

dear Officer Jones

Thank you for visiting our classroom.
We posted your safety tips on the wall. Stay safe.

yours truly,

Ms. Berger's class

_____

_____

_____

_____

_____

© Macmillan/McGraw-Hill

At Home: Have your child write a letter and then review it for correct letter punctuation.

Name _____

- Add ***-ed*** to most verbs to tell about an action in the past.
- If a verb ends with one consonant, double the consonant and add ***-ed***.
- If a verb ends with ***-e***, drop the ***e*** and add ***-ed***.

Find the mistakes in the letter. Rewrite it correctly below.

dear Emily

Our teacher planed an awesome trip to the museum. We learnned all about dinosaurs. We watchd a movie about Tyrannosaurus Rex. We were most surprised to see real dinosaur fossils.

your friend

Carlos

_____

_____

_____

_____

_____

_____

© Macmillan/McGraw-Hill

At Home: Ask your child to write a letter about an event or trip that happened in the past.

Name _____

Rewrite each sentence to tell about the past. Change the underlined verb to the past tense.

1. The men and women work as a team.

_____

2. They hunt for dinosaur bones in the desert sand.

_____

3. One man rams his shovel into something hard.

_____

4. He waves to the other members of his team.

_____

5. Two women carefully pick up the dinosaur bones.

_____

6. They ship the bones home in a crate.

_____

7. Later, scientists examine the bones closely.

_____

8. They learn the size and shape of the dinosaur.

_____

© Macmillan/McGraw-Hill

At Home: Review this page together.

Name _____

- The verb ***have*** has a special form in the present tense.
- Use ***has*** when the subject is singular.

  Pete has tap shoes.
- Use ***have*** when the subject is plural or ***I*** or ***you***.

  Marta and Joe have top hats.

  I have a cane.

Complete each sentence with *has* or *have*.

1. We _____ a school play in the winter.
2. My brother _____ a singing part.
3. My friends Lily and Sam _____ talking parts.
4. I _____ a flute that I play in the band.
5. My teacher _____ a clarinet.
6. We all _____ a great time putting on the play.

Write one sentence with *has*. Write another sentence with *have*. Write them on the lines below.

7. _____

_____

8. _____

_____

© Macmillan/McGraw-Hill

At Home: Have your child tell about some things in his or her rooms.

Name _____

- The past-tense form of ***have*** is ***had***.
- Use ***had*** in the past tense with any subject.

I had a dance recital.

My friends had fun watching me dance.

Change the verb *have* from present tense to past tense in each sentence. Write the new sentence on the lines.

1. We have our dance show in January.

_____

2. The show has three parts.

_____

3. I have a lead role.

_____

4. Juanita has a solo.

_____

5. We have a party after the show.

_____

© Macmillan/McGraw-Hill

At Home: Ask your child to write sentences using the past-tense form of the verb *have*.

Name _____

- Begin the first word and each important word in a book title with a capital letter.
- Underline the title of a book.

A Very Young Dancer

Olivia Saves the Circus

Correct the underlined book title in each sentence. Write it correctly on the line below.

1. chasing vermeer is a book about a famous painting.

_____

2. I just finished reading a book called polly and the piano.

_____

3. the little ballerina is my sister's favorite picture book.

_____

4. We read the kids' guide to acting and stagecraft to prepare for our school play.

_____

5. The library has a funny book called angelina, star of the show.

_____

© Macmillan/McGraw-Hill

At Home: Have your child write a sentence telling about a book he or she read recently.

Name _____

- Use ***has*** in the present tense when the subject is singular. Use ***have*** when the subject is plural or ***I*** or ***you***.
- The past-tense form of ***have*** is ***had***.
- Capitalize the first letter and each important word in a book title. Underline the whole title.

Circle the mistakes in the sentences. Write the sentences correctly on the lines.

1. Our class is making a play of the book charlie and the chocolate factory.

_____

_____

2. We have tryouts yesterday.

_____

3. Alison have a great singing voice.

_____

4. Three boys has the part of Charlie.

_____

5. You has to come see our show!

_____

© Macmillan/McGraw-Hill

At Home: Have your child write two sentences about favorite books.

Name _____

Circle the correct form of the verb *have* to complete each sentence.

1. My best friend Kim and I (have, has) big dreams.
2. Kim (have, has) dreams of being a singer on Broadway.
3. Even as a baby, she (has, had) a good voice.
4. Her dreams (have, has) a good chance of coming true.
5. Today, I (have, had) a dream of playing in a rock band.
6. My father (have, has) his old guitar in the garage.
7. He and his pals (have, had) a rock band a long time ago.
8. One of his friends (have, has) a music studio in the city.
9. Last week, I (have, had) my first lesson there.
10. I (have, has) a lot to learn before my first show.

© Macmillan/McGraw-Hill

At Home: Review this page together.

Name _____

- If two sentences have words that are the same, you can combine them.
- You can combine sentences by joining words with ***and***.

The horses eat hay. The horses play in the field.

The horses eat hay and play in the field.

Combine each pair of sentences by using the word *and*. Write the new sentence on the line.

1. **a.** The cows live in the barn.
   b. The horses live in the barn.

   _____

   _____

2. **a.** Farmer Brown wakes up early.
   b. Farmer Brown goes to bed early.

   _____

   _____

3. **a.** Mrs. Brown plants corn.
   b. Mrs. Brown eats corn.

   _____

   _____

4. **a.** The children milk the cows.
   b. The children feed the chickens.

   _____

   _____

© Macmillan/McGraw-Hill

At Home: Have your child write pairs of sentences that have some of the same words and then combine them.

Name _____

- If sentences have subjects that are the same, you can combine them.
- Sometimes you can combine sentences by joining two predicates with ***and***.

The cow slept. The cow ate.

The cow slept and ate.

Combine each pair of sentences by joining the predicates with the word *and*. Write the new sentences on the lines.

1. **a.** The cows walk in the field.
   b. The cows eat grass.

   _____

2. **a.** The farmer sits on a stool.
   b. The farmer milks the cow.

   _____

3. **a.** The pigs roll in the mud.
   b. The pigs get dirty.

   _____

4. **a.** The barn is big.
   b. The barn has red sides.

   _____

© Macmillan/McGraw-Hill

At Home: Have your child act out two actions and then say sentences that combine them.

Name _____

- End statements and commands with a period.
- End a question with a question mark.
- End an exclamation with an exclamation mark.

Who will feed the pigs? Sarah will feed the pigs.

Feed the pigs now. Oh no, I spilled the food!

Read each sentence and add the correct punctuation.

1. Did you hear the rooster _____
2. Wake up and get dressed _____
3. I'm so tired _____
4. What's for breakfast _____
5. Please feed the chickens _____
6. I like to feed the animals _____
7. Which animal do you like best _____
8. The piglets are so cute _____
9. Who will clean the chicken coop _____
10. The chicken coop is a mess _____

© Macmillan/McGraw-Hill

At Home: Have your child write four sentences and use the correct punctuation marks.

Name _____

- Sometimes you can combine sentences by joining two predicates with ***and***.
- End a statement or a command with a period.
- End a question with a question mark.
- End an exclamation with an exclamation mark.

Rewrite the paragraph correctly on the lines below. Add punctuation and combine sentences with the same subjects.

Have you ever been to a farm Our class went on a trip to a farm. Our class saw lots of animals. We watched baby chicks hop around We watched pigs play in the mud Boy, did those pigs get dirty

_____

_____

_____

_____

_____

© Macmillan/McGraw-Hill

At Home: Have your child add a second paragraph about the class trip to the farm.

Name _____

Circle the parts of the sentences that can be combined with the word *and*. Combine the sentences. Write the new sentence on the line.

1. Most farmers get up before dawn.
   Most farmers work until sunset.

   _____

   _____

2. Farm children do chores before school.
   Farm children do chores after school.

   _____

   _____

3. Beans grow in the field.
   Tomatoes grow in the field.

   _____

   _____

4. The crops need water to grow.
   The crops need sunlight to grow.

   _____

   _____

5. People stop at the farm stand.
   People buy freshly picked corn.

   _____

   _____

© Macmillan/McGraw-Hill

At Home: Review this page together.

Name _____

- A **linking verb** is a verb that does not show action.
- The verb ***be*** is a linking verb.
- The verb ***be*** has special forms in the present tense (***is, are, am***).

  The panda bear is cute. Pelicans are birds.

  I am at the zoo.

Write *am, is,* or *are* to complete each sentence.

1. Mammals _____ warm-blooded.
2. A cow _____ a mammal.
3. Dolphins _____ mammals, too.
4. I _____ a mammal!
5. Cows _____ plant eaters.
6. A dolphin _____ a meat eater.
7. I _____ a meat eater, too.
8. What _____ your favorite kind of mammal?

© Macmillan/McGraw-Hill

At Home: Have your child tell the location of household objects using ***is*** and ***are***.

Name _____

- The past-tense form for ***am*** is ***was.***
- The past-tense form for ***is*** is ***was.***
- The past-tense form for ***are*** is ***were.***

I am at the park. Yesterday, I was at the farm.
The chick is in the yard. Earlier, it was in the barn.
The bears are sleepy. In the spring, they were active.

Choose the correct linking verb in ( ). Then write the complete sentence below.

1. Yesterday I (was, were) in the woods.

_____

2. There (was, were) a deer eating leaves.

_____

3. The birds (was, were) in the air.

_____

4. A squirrel (was, were) up in a tree.

_____

5. It (was, were) very peaceful.

_____

© Macmillan/McGraw-Hill

At Home: Have your child use linking verbs to describe a place he or she visited in the past.

Name _____

- A proper noun begins with a capital letter.
- The name of a day, month, or holiday begins with a capital letter.

My dog Ralph had puppies in June.

Find capitalization mistakes in the sentences. Write the corrected sentences on the lines below.

1. memorial day was last monday.

_____

2. molly jones went fishing with her family.

_____

3. The month of may is a nice time to go fishing.

_____

4. Molly's brother ted caught a bass.

_____

5. Mr. jones fried the fish for lunch on tuesday.

_____

© Macmillan/McGraw-Hill

At Home: Have your child write sentences about different activities he or she does each day of the week.

Name _____

- The words ***is, are, am was,*** and ***were*** can be linking verbs.

Read the paragraph and find the mistakes. Rewrite the passage correctly on the lines below.

Brown bears is one of the largest types of bears. A female brown bear are about half the size of a male. These bears has thick fur that are usually brown. Some bears is lighter, and others is almost black. Brown bear cubs are born between january and march.

_____

_____

_____

_____

_____

© Macmillan/McGraw-Hill

At Home: Have your child write a paragraph about a familiar animal and point out each use of a linking verb.

Name _____

Circle the present form of the verb *be* in each sentence. Rewrite the sentence. Change the verb to past tense.

1. I am at the kitchen window.

_____

2. The leaves of the maple tree are bright red.

_____

3. A chipmunk is in the grass.

_____

4. Its nest is under the ground.

_____

5. Some nuts and seeds are on the grass.

_____

6. The chipmunk's cheeks are full.

_____

© Macmillan/McGraw-Hill

At Home: Review this page together.

Name _____

- A **helping verb** helps another verb show an action.
- ***Have*** and ***has*** can be helping verbs.

  The bear has found berries.

  The birds have built a nest.

Write *has* or *have* to complete each sentence.

1. The mother bird _____ been searching for food.
2. She _____ found worms for her chicks.
3. The chicks _____ eaten the worms.
4. Oh no, the nest _____ fallen out of the tree!
5. Some foxes _____ spotted the nest.
6. I hope those foxes _____ already had their lunch!
7. The mother bird _____ tried to protect her chicks.
8. The chicks _____ escaped!

© Macmillan/McGraw-Hill

At Home: Have your child write sentences using the helping verbs ***has*** and ***have***.

Name _____

- A **helping verb** helps another verb show an action.
- ***Is, are, am, was,*** and ***were*** can be helping verbs.

  A fox is looking for food.
  The bears are hibernating.
  I am watching the birds fly south.
  The squirrels were gathering nuts.

Choose the correct helping verb in ( ). Then write the complete sentence below.

1. The chicks (was, were) following their mother.

_____

2. The mother bird (was, were) protecting her babies.

_____

3. One chick (is, are) pecking around for food.

_____

4. Another chick (is, are) hiding behind its mother.

_____

5. I (am, are) watching the chicks.

_____

© Macmillan/McGraw-Hill

At Home: Have your child make up oral sentences using helping verbs ***is***, ***are***, ***am***, ***was***, and ***were***.

Name _____

- Quotation marks set off the exact words that a person says.
- Use quotation marks at the beginning and end of what a person says.

  "Do you see the rabbit?" asked Noah.

Find the mistakes in the sentences. Write the corrected sentences on the lines below.

1. I see the rabbit, said Ben.

   _____

2. Noah said, It's so fast!

   _____

3. Where is it going? asked Kim.

   _____

4. It's going into the garden, replied Noah.

   _____

5. Ben asked Do you think it's hungry?

   _____

6. Let's follow it! said Kim.

   _____

© Macmillan/McGraw-Hill

At Home: Have your child write a sentence that includes the exact words of a person.

Name _____

- ***Have, has, is, are, am, was,*** and ***were*** can be helping verbs.
- Use quotation marks at the beginning and end of what a person says.

Read the paragraph and find the mistakes. Rewrite the passage correctly on the lines below.

In school we is learning about gorillas. Gorillas are large and gentle apes said our teacher. We read that they live in africa. We has also learned that gorillas eat vegetables. I is excited to learn more about gorillas.

_____

_____

_____

_____

_____

_____

_____

© Macmillan/McGraw-Hill

At **Home:** Have your child write about something he or she is learning in school. Ask him or her to use helping verbs.

Name _____

Fill in the circle for the correct helping verb and then write it in the blank to complete each sentence.

1. The whales _____ been searching for food.
   - ○ have
   - ○ has
   - ○ is
   - ○ are
2. People _____ fishing in the same part of the sea.
   - ○ has
   - ○ am
   - ○ have
   - ○ are
3. A fishing line _____ become stuck in a whale's jaw.
   - ○ is
   - ○ has
   - ○ were
   - ○ am
4. The whale can't eat and _____ getting weak.
   - ○ have
   - ○ am
   - ○ is
   - ○ are
5. People _____ working hard to help the whale.
   - ○ were
   - ○ have
   - ○ has
   - ○ is
6. They _____ untangled the line and saved the whale.
   - ○ has
   - ○ am
   - ○ are
   - ○ have

© Macmillan/McGraw-Hill

At Home: Review this page together.

Name _____

- Some verbs do not have ***-ed*** in the past tense.
- The verbs ***go*** and ***do*** have special forms in the past tense.

I, we, you, they	go	went
I, we, you, they	do	did

Choose the correct verb in ( ). Then write the complete sentence below.

1. Our class (go, went) to the library to learn about pollution.

_____

_____

2. Last year we (do, did) a lot to stop pollution.

_____

3. Toxic wastes should not (go, went) into the ocean.

_____

4. What (do, did) you do to stop pollution last year?

_____

5. Last summer we (go, went) to clean-up day at the beach.

_____

_____

6. Everyone (do, did) a lot of work picking up trash.

_____

© Macmillan/McGraw-Hill

At Home: Have your child write sentences that use ***go, went, do,*** and ***did***.

Name _____

- The verbs ***say*** and ***see*** have special forms in the past tense.

I, we, you, they	see	saw
I, we, you, they	say	said

Rewrite the sentences using the past tense of the verb in dark type.

1. I **see** a boy litter.

_____

2. I **say** "Don't pollute!"

_____

3. We **see** him pick up his garbage.

_____

4. "Thank you!" we **say**.

_____

5. The children **see** lots of people litter.

_____

6. "Clean up!" the children **say** to all of them.

_____

© Macmillan/McGraw-Hill

At Home: Have your child write sentences with the irregular verbs ***saw*** and ***said.***

Name _____

- Capitalize the greeting and closing in a letter.
- Use a comma after the greeting and closing in a letter.
- Use a comma between the day and the year in a date.
- Use a comma between the names of a city and a state.

Find the mistakes in the letter. Write the corrected letter on the lines below.

42 Elm Road
Atlanta Georgia
May 9 2007

dear Rachel

We are going to Hawaii on june 6 2007. We will visit a rain forest. Do you want to go with us?

your pal
Elena

_____

_____

_____

_____

_____

© Macmillan/McGraw-Hill

At Home: Have your child write a letter to a friend or family member.

Name _____

- The verbs ***go, do, say,*** and ***see*** have special forms in the past tense.
- Capitalize the greeting and closing in a letter.
- Use a comma after the greeting and closing in a letter.
- Use a comma between the day and the year in a date.
- Use a comma between the names of a city and a state.

Read the letter. Find the mistakes. Rewrite it correctly.

4 Quaker Lane
Tyler Texas
March 8 2008

dear Grandma Rose

Our class go to the planetarium last tuesday. "Venus is very hot," say our teacher. What planets does you know about?

love
Angela

_____

_____

_____

_____

© Macmillan/McGraw-Hill

At Home: Have your child write a letter that uses the past tense of ***go, do, say,*** and ***see***.

Name _____

Write the past tense of the verb in ( ) to complete each sentence.

1. I _____ a movie about helping our planet. (see)

2. Our teacher _____ we have to change bad habits. (say)

3. Mark, _____ you see the dripping faucet? (do)

4. The water _____ down the drain and was wasted. (go)

5. Mom _____ that the TV was on, but we weren't there. (see)

6. All the children _____ to bed. (go)

7. They _____ they forgot to turn off the TV. (say)

8. In the past, we _____ many things without thinking. (do)

© Macmillan/McGraw-Hill

At Home: Review this page together.

Name _____

- Some verbs do not have ***-ed*** in the past tense.
- The verbs ***come*** and ***run*** have special forms in the past tense.

I, we, you, they	come	came
I, we, you, they	run	ran

Circle the correct verb in ( ) to complete each sentence.

1. Mark (comed, came) home when the storm began.
2. The rain (comed, came) down fast and hard.
3. I (ran, runned) home quickly, too.
4. On his way, Mark (ran, runned) into a store.
5. Emily and Tia (come, came) into the store, too.
6. Together they (runned, ran) through the raindrops.
7. When they (came, come) inside, they were soaking wet.
8. Mark and I (runned, ran) to get towels.

© Macmillan/McGraw-Hill

At Home: Have your child write sentences with the verbs ***ran*** and ***came.***

Name _____

- Some verbs do not have ***-ed*** in the past tense.
- The verbs ***give*** and ***sing*** have special forms in the past tense.

I, we, you, they	give	gave
I, we, you, they	sing	sang

Change the words in dark type to past tense. Write the new sentence on the line below.

1. I **sing** the song about raindrops.

_____

2. I **give** my old snow boots to my little brother.

_____

3. We **sing** in a high voice.

_____

4. They **sing** in a low voice.

_____

5. We **give** our winter coats to charity.

_____

6. You **give** money for hurricane victims, too.

_____

© Macmillan/McGraw-Hill

At Home: Say a sentence with ***give*** or ***sing.*** Ask your child to turn the sentence into the past tense.

Name _____

- Begin the first word and each important word in a book title with a capital letter.
- Underline all the words in the title of a book.

  Flash, Crash, Rumble, and Roll

  Feel the Wind

Correct the underlined book title in each sentence. Write the title correctly on the line below.

1. I read **the kids' book of weather forecasting** to learn about weather.

   _____

2. **feel the wind** is a book about what causes wind.

   _____

3. The book **rain tonight** is about a real hurricane.

   _____

4. Charlie loves the book **night of the twisters** by Ivy Ruckman.

   _____

5. To learn about volcanoes, read **forces of nature**.

   _____

© Macmillan/McGraw-Hill

At Home: Have your child write about a book and write its title correctly.

Name _____

- The verbs ***come, run, give,*** and ***sing*** have special forms in the past tense.
- Begin the first word and each important word in a book title with a capital letter.
- Underline all the words in the title of a book.

Read the paragraph and find the mistakes. Rewrite the passage correctly on the lines below.

Only two friends comed to my party because of the blizzard. We runned around in the snow and had fun. One friend give me a book called blizzards and ice storms. What a perfect present, I said. Then they singed Happy Birthday to me, and we ate cake.

_____

_____

_____

_____

_____

_____

© Macmillan/McGraw-Hill

At Home: Have your child write about a rainy or snowy day in the past and include some irregular verbs.

Name _____

Make a check [✓] next to a sentence if the underlined past tense verb is correct. Make an X if the verb is not correct.

1. This morning we singed a song about the weather.
2. Then Matt and Meytal gave the daily weather report.
3. The heavy rain that came in overnight will stop by noon.
4. That gived us a chance to go outside.
5. After lunch we runned around in the schoolyard.
6. A small yellow bird sang sweetly from a tree.
7. The sun comed out from behind the clouds.
8. Paul ran and jumped over the large puddles.

Rewrite the sentences you marked X correctly on the lines.

_____

_____

_____

_____

© Macmillan/McGraw-Hill

At Home: Review this page together.

Name _____

- A **contraction** is a short form of two words.
- An **apostrophe** (') takes the place of the letters that are left out.

is not	isn't	are not	aren't
has not	hasn't	have not	haven't

Replace the underlined words with contractions. Write the new sentences on the lines.

1. The Arctic is not at the South Pole.

_____

2. The Arctic is not warm.

_____

3. There are not any trees in the Arctic.

_____

4. I have not been to the Arctic.

_____

5. Glen has not been there either.

_____

6. Are you not going to the Arctic next summer?

_____

© Macmillan/McGraw-Hill

At Home: Write ***is not, are not, has not,*** and ***have not,*** and have your child write the contraction for each one.

Name _____

- A **contraction** is a short form of two words.
- An **apostrophe** (') takes the place of the letters that are left out.
- ***Doesn't, don't, didn't,*** and ***can't*** are contractions.

does not	doesn't	do not	don't
did not	didn't	can not	can't

Replace the underlined words with contractions. Write the new sentences on the lines.

1. Many animals can not live in the Arctic.

_____

2. They do not do well in the cold weather.

_____

3. Most birds can not live in the Arctic all year.

_____

4. The tern does not stay for the winter.

_____

5. Do not be afraid of the Arctic wolf.

_____

6. The Arctic hare did not see the wolf.

_____

© Macmillan/McGraw-Hill

At Home: Write ***doesn't, don't, didn't,*** and ***can't,*** and have your child write the two words in each contraction.

Name _____

- A contraction is a short form of two words.
- An apostrophe (') takes the place of the letters that are left out.

Add the apostrophe to each contraction. Write the contraction correctly on the line.

1. Living in the Arctic isnt easy. _____
2. Most animals arent adapted to life in the Arctic. _____
3. Arctic wolf pups cant see or hear. _____
4. The cold doesnt get through the polar bear's thick fur.

   _____

5. Some Arctic animals arent easy to see in the snow.

   _____

6. Arctic hares dont want to run into a wolf. _____
7. The muskox isnt friendly with the wolf. _____
8. We didnt see the walrus come out of the water. _____

© Macmillan/McGraw-Hill

At Home: Have your child create sentences using contractions.

Name _____

- A contraction is a short form of two words.
- An apostrophe (') takes the place of the letters that are left out of a contraction.

Read the paragraph and find the contraction and punctuation mistakes. Rewrite the paragraph correctly on the lines below.

In the book the lives of arctic animals, I read that Arctic animals dont get cold. It isnt' just a book about animals. I also learned that the sun does'nt come out in the winter at the North Pole. Did you know that there ar'ent any trees in the Arctic?

_____

_____

_____

_____

_____

_____

© Macmillan/McGraw-Hill

At Home: Have your child write a summary of a book recently read. Encourage him or her to use contractions.

Name _____

Underline two words in each sentence that could be used to form a contraction. Then write the contractions on the lines below.

1. Some animals do not stay awake in cold weather.
2. The bears have not been awake for most of the winter.
3. A bear's heartbeat is not as fast while it sleeps.
4. There are not a lot of things for bears to eat in winter.
5. The bear does not need to eat during this time.
6. It has not used up all the energy stored in its body fat.
7. Other animals can not go so long without food.
8. I did not know that snakes and frogs sleep in winter.

1. _____ 2. _____

3. _____ 4. _____

5. _____ 6. _____

7. _____ 8. _____

© Macmillan/McGraw-Hill

At Home: Review this page together.

Name _____

- A **pronoun** is a word that takes the place of a noun or nouns.
- A pronoun must agree with the noun it replaces.
- The pronouns ***I, he, she, it,*** and ***you*** can take the place of a singular noun.

She touched the desert sand. It was very hot.
Do you know where the desert is? I know where it is.
He knows where the desert is, too.

Circle a pronoun to replace the underlined noun in each sentence.

1. Mina went on a trip to the Mohave Desert. She It
2. The desert was hot and dry. He It
3. Mina's brother saw a cactus. He It
4. The cactus was green and prickly. He It
5. Mina saw a Gila Monster! She He
6. Did you know that a Gila Monster is a lizard? she it
7. Mina was scared! It She
8. Mina's dad was a little scared, too. He She

© Macmillan/McGraw-Hill

At Home: Have your child write about what else Mina and her family saw using ***I, he, she, it,*** and ***you***.

Name _____

- A **plural noun** names more than one person, place, or thing.
- **Pronouns *we, you,*** and ***they*** can take the place of a plural noun or more than one noun or pronoun.

Rattlesnakes are dangerous.	They are dangerous
Emma and I saw a rattlesnake.	We saw a rattlesnake.

Circle the correct pronoun in ( ) to complete each sentence.

1. Jamal and Nora are going to catch the snakes. We're glad (you, she) are here, Jamal and Nora!
2. Now (we, I) are safe!
3. Did you hear the wolves? (We, They) are howling.
4. Wolves don't eat people, so (we, she) are not in danger.
5. Mom and I hope to see wolf pups. (They, He) are so cute!
6. Have (you, she) ever seen a wolf pup?
7. How big does (it, they) grow?
8. (I, We) are having so much fun in the desert.

© Macmillan/McGraw-Hill

At Home: In the sentences above, have your child write the plural noun that each pronoun replaces.

Name _____

- **Quotation marks** set off the exact words of a speaker.
- Use quotation marks (“ ”) at the beginning and end of what a person says.

  “How hot is the desert?” asked Lydia.

Read the sentences. Write the sentences correctly on the lines.

1. Where is the Sahara Desert? asked Maria.

   _____

2. It is in Africa, said Ms. Jackson.

   _____

3. The Sahara is the largest desert! said our teacher.

   _____

4. How big is the Sahara Desert? asked Jared.

   _____

5. It covers 3,500,000 square miles! said Ms. Jackson.

   _____

6. Which desert is the smallest? Ms. Jackson asked us.

   _____

7. Where is the smallest desert? asked James.

   _____

8. It’s in Canada, said Ms. Jackson.

   _____

© Macmillan/McGraw-Hill

At Home: Have your child work with you to write your own dialogues using quotation marks.

Name _____

- A pronoun must agree with the noun it replaces.

Find each mistake. Then rewrite the paragraphs correctly on the lines below.

Mr. Walker taught the class what him knows about desert plants. She said, The desert is home to many plants. How can they grow in dry deserts?

Some desert plants store water in their roots, said Leah.

She are right! said Mr. Walker.

_____

_____

_____

_____

_____

_____

_____

© Macmillan/McGraw-Hill

At Home: Have your child record a simple dialog and then proofread it.

Name _____

Mark the pronoun that could replace the underlined words.

1. Ruby is in the first car with Dad and Seth.
   O They O She O I O We
2. Mom and the two younger boys were in the other car.
   O I O They O It O He
3. Mr. Ali will be our guide through the desert.
   O She O They O He O It
4. Anna was surprised to see so many flowers and plants.
   O I O They O It O He
5. "The desert is not a dead place," Mr. Ali said.
   O You O It O He O We
6. Ruby and I took pictures of the giant cactus.
   O We O She O It O He
7. The giant cactus had branches that looked like arms.
   O You O We O It O They
8. Ruby and Anna can eat the fruit of the giant cactus.
   O It O She O I O You

© Macmillan/McGraw-Hill

At Home: Review this page together.

Name _____

- Use ***I*** in the subject part of the sentence.
- Use ***me*** in the predicate part of the sentence.
- Name yourself last when talking about yourself and another person.

  I have a dancing part in the show.

  The teacher helps me learn the steps.

Write *I* or *me* to complete each sentence.

1. Isabel and _____ are trying out for a play.
2. The director calls _____ in first.
3. Isabel wishes _____ luck.
4. _____ am so nervous!
5. The director asks _____ to read from a script.
6. After I read, he thanks _____.
7. Next he asks _____ to sing a song.
8. Isabel and _____ hope we get parts in the play.

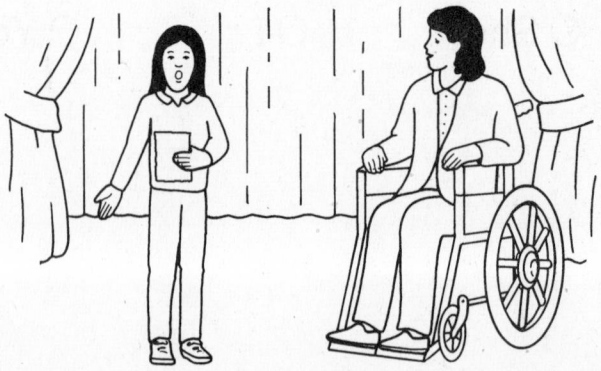

© Macmillan/McGraw-Hill

At Home: Have your child identify each pronoun written above as a subject or part of a predicate.

Name _____

- Use ***we*** and ***us*** when you talk about yourself and another person.
- Use ***we*** in the subject part of the sentence.
- Use ***us*** in the predicate part.

We will wear tutus in the dance show.

Mom will help us make our costumes.

Replace the underlined words with *we* or *us*. Write the new sentence on the line below.

1. Jackie and I love to dance!

_____

2. Our teacher asked Jackie and me to dance in the school play.

_____

3. Jackie and I will learn all the steps.

_____

4. Jackie and I will practice every day.

_____

5. The audience will like Jackie and me.

_____

6. They will throw roses at Jackie and me.

_____

© Macmillan/McGraw-Hill

At Home: Have your child write two more sentences about the dancers described in the sentences above.

Name _____

- The pronoun ***I*** is always a capital letter.
- Use ***I*** in the subject of a sentence.

Correct the sentences and write them on the lines.

1. i was the king in the school play.

_____

2. Mara and i sang a song together.

_____

3. i had many lines to learn.

_____

4. The queen and i danced together.

_____

5. At the end of the play, i took a bow.

_____

6. Matt and i went for ice cream after the play.

_____

© Macmillan/McGraw-Hill

At Home: Have your child write sentences about him or herself and then underline the word ***I*** in each sentence.

Name _____

- Use ***I*** and ***we*** in the subject of a sentence.
- Use ***me*** and ***us*** in the predicate part of a sentence.
- The pronoun ***I*** is always a capital letter.
- Name yourself last when talking about yourself and another person.

Circle each mistake in the use of pronouns. Then rewrite the paragraph correctly on the lines below.

Mom and me went to see a musical. The usher gave i a program and showed we where to sit. Us had great seats! i could see the actors right up close. i hope Mom takes I to another show soon!

_____

_____

_____

_____

_____

_____

© Macmillan/McGraw-Hill

At Home: Have your child write a paragraph that includes the pronouns ***I, me, we,*** and ***us***.

Name _____

Write C if the underlined pronoun is correct. If the pronoun is not correct, cross it out and write the correct pronoun on the line.

1. What play do you think us should put on? _____
2. I would like to write a new play. _____
3. Henry and me would like to help you. _____
4. They asked Hasheem and I to make the set. _____
5. Would you like we to work on the costumes? _____
6. Tomorrow Ann and me will print the programs. _____
7. Can someone help Joe and I with our lines? _____
8. We can't wait until opening night. _____
9. The audience clapped a long time for us. _____
10. Next year the kids and I want to do a musical. _____

© Macmillan/McGraw-Hill

At Home: Review this page together.

Name _____

- A **possessive pronoun** takes the place of a possessive noun.
- A possessive pronoun shows who or what owns something.
- ***My, your, his,*** and ***her*** are possessive pronouns.

This is my globe. This is your map.

Where is his house? Here is her car.

Circle the correct possessive pronoun in ( ) for each sentence. Write it on the line.

1. (Me, My) favorite explorer is Christopher Columbus. _____
2. (His, He) ships were called the *Niña, Pinta,* and *Santa Maria.*

   _____
3. (Him, His) journey was very long. _____
4. I followed it on (my, me) map. _____
5. Sacajawea is (your, you) favorite explorer. _____
6. (She, Her) journey was very important in U.S. history.

   _____
7. Sacajawea tied (her, she) baby to her back. _____
8. Did you trace (her, she) journey on the map? _____

© Macmillan/McGraw-Hill

At Home: Have your child use possessive pronouns to describe things belonging to others.

Name _____

- A **possessive pronoun** shows who or what owns something. Some possessive pronouns are ***its, our, your, their.***

Our house is on Elm Street. Their house is on Oak Street.

Your house is pretty. Its color is pink.

Underline the correct possessive pronouns. Write the sentences correctly on the lines.

1. (Us, Our) class is learning about Alexander Graham Bell and Thomas Watson.

_____

2. (Their, They) invention changed the way we live.

_____

3. Can you imagine (your, our) life without a telephone?

_____

4. (It's, Its) technology helps us to stay in touch.

_____

5. What inventor will (our, its) teacher tell us about next?

_____

6. What is (your, you're) favorite invention?

_____

© Macmillan/McGraw-Hill

At Home: Have your child write sentences using the possessive pronouns ***its, our, your,*** and ***their.***

Name _____

- A proper noun begins with a capital letter.
- The name of a day, month, or holiday begins with a capital letter.

  Columbus Day is the second Monday in October.

Find the mistakes. Write the corrected sentences on the lines.

1. colorado was the first state to observe columbus day.

   _____

   _____

2. memorial day is the last monday in may.

   _____

3. Both abraham lincoln and george washington were both born in february.

   _____

   _____

4. The third monday in february is presidents' day.

   _____

   _____

5. President truman declared june 14 flag day.

   _____

6. I was born on sunday, august 17.

   _____

© Macmillan/McGraw-Hill

At Home: Have your child write sentences about holidays. Remind him or her to use capital letters.

Name _____

- A possessive pronoun takes the place of a possessive noun.
- A possessive pronoun shows who or what owns something. Some possessive pronouns are ***my, your, his, its, our, your,*** and ***their.***
- A proper noun begins with a capital letter.
- The name of a day, month, or holiday begins with a capital letter.

Find the mistakes. Rewrite the paragraph correctly on the lines below.

Me twin brothers have a birthday on presidents' day. There party is on saturday, february 18. Us parents got the boys a puppy as a present. Their name is gus. Gus will sleep in them room.

_____

_____

_____

_____

_____

© Macmillan/McGraw-Hill

At Home: Have your child name objects and their owners and then supply the correct possessive pronouns.

Name _____

Underline the possessive pronoun that completes each sentence correctly. Write it on the line.

1. "This is _____ new invention," said Sammy.
   my me I
2. "_____ invention is a very strange looking thing," Tito said.
   Your Its Our
3. "Where is _____ on and off switch?" Kayla asked.
   me you its
4. Kayla wanted to show off _____ own invention next.
   she her its
5. Sammy put _____ hand on the small black switch.
   his you me
6. "Should we all cover _____ eyes?" Ina asked.
   her my our
7. To be safe, the kids moved _____ chairs back.
   its their they
8. "Hold on to _____ hats, kids!" Sammy said with a grin.
   your its their

© Macmillan/McGraw-Hill

At Home: Review this page together.

Name _____

- A present-tense verb must agree with a pronoun in the subject part of a sentence.
- With the pronouns ***he, she,*** and ***it,*** add ***-s*** to most verbs to form the present tense.

  He picks a flower. She smells the rose. It smells great.

Underline the verbs that agree with the pronouns. Write the sentences on the lines.

1. She (want, wants) to plant a garden.

   _____

2. It (takes, take) hard work to plant a garden.

   _____

3. She (buys, buy) seeds at the store.

   _____

4. He (help, helps) her plant the seeds.

   _____

5. He (waters, water) the garden.

   _____

6. It (look, looks) good.

   _____

© Macmillan/McGraw-Hill

At Home: Have your child write sentences using ***she, he,*** and ***it.***

Name _____

- Remember that a present-tense verb must agree with its pronoun subject.
- With the pronouns ***I, we, you,*** and ***they,*** do **not** add ***-s*** to most action verbs to form the present tense.

We visit your garden. You show us around.

I pick some tomatoes. They taste great!

Circle the pronoun in ( ) that agrees with the verb in each sentence.

1. (You, She) enjoy gardening.
2. (We, He) think your garden is lovely.
3. What kind of flowers do (you, she) grow?
4. (I, He) see red roses.
5. (It, They) grow so tall!
6. How do (she, you) grow such pretty flowers?
7. (I, He) want to take some flowers home.
8. Can (we, us) pick the roses?

© Macmillan/McGraw-Hill

At Home: Have your child write sentences using ***I, we, you,*** and ***they.***

Name _____

- Underline all the words in the title of a book.
- Begin the first word and each important word in a book title with a capital letter.
- Any unimportant word in a book title, such as ***a, and, for, of, the,*** and ***to*** should **not** begin with a capital letter unless it is the first word in the title.

The Giant Carrot The Big Book of Gardening

Correct the book titles in the sentences. Write the titles correctly on the lines below.

1. In the book carlos and the squash plant, a squash grows out of a boy's ear!

_____

2. The book The Gardener won the Caldecott Honor Award.

_____

3. I read the book planting a rainbow to my little brother.

_____

4. From Seed to Plant is about how to grow a bean plant.

_____

5. How a seed grows tells how an acorn grows into an oak tree.

_____

© Macmillan/McGraw-Hill

At Home: Have your child write a sentence about a book he or she has read.

Name _____

- With the pronouns ***he, she,*** and ***it,*** add ***-s*** to most action verbs to form the present tense.
- With the pronouns ***I, we, you,*** and ***they,*** do **not** add ***-s*** to most action verbs to form the present tense.
- Begin the first word and all the important words in a book title with capital letters.
- Underline all the words in a book title.

Find the mistakes. Rewrite the paragraph correctly.

Mom and I goes to the library. She read how to grow a garden. I reads A Kid's Guide to Gardening. The books tells us how to grow a garden. We wants to plant flowers. We knows it take hard work.

_____

_____

_____

_____

_____

_____

© Macmillan/McGraw-Hill

At Home: Have your child continue the paragraph and then proofread it.

Name _____

Underline the pronoun subject in each sentence. Then rewrite the sentence. Make the present-tense verb agree with its pronoun subject.

1. We plants a garden in early spring.

_____

2. Do you thinks vegetables will grow well here?

_____

3. For a while, it seem that nothing happens.

_____

4. They waits patiently, and soon green shoots appear.

_____

5. One day I sees some white blossoms.

_____

6. Then he say, "Look, peppers are growing."

_____

7. They grows quickly under the warm sun.

_____

8. She pick peppers, peas, and lettuce.

_____

© Macmillan/McGraw-Hill

At Home: Review this page together.

Name _____

- A **contraction** is a short form of two words put together.
- An apostrophe (') takes the place of the letter or letters that are left out.
- Some contractions are formed by putting together pronouns and verbs.

I am I'm she is she's he is he's

Write the contraction for the underlined words in each sentence.

1. I am looking at the moon. _____
2. He is gazing at the stars. _____
3. She is an astronaut. _____
4. I am very interested in the moon. _____
5. He is going to teach me about the stars. _____

Write the two words that were put together to form each contraction.

6. She's flying to the moon. _____
7. He's going with her. _____
8. I'm going to fly to the moon one day. _____

© Macmillan/McGraw-Hill

At Home: Have your child write more sentences using the contractions ***I'm, he's,*** and ***she's.***

Name _____

- A **contraction** is a short form of two words put together.
- An apostrophe (') takes the place of the missing letter or letters in the contraction.

it is	it's	we are	we're
they are	they're	you are	you're

Write the contraction for the underlined words.
Write the new sentence on the lines.

1. It is a starry night. _____

_____

2. We are gazing at the stars. _____

_____

3. They are beautiful! _____

_____

4. It is going to be nice tomorrow. _____

_____

5. You are reading books about stars. _____

_____

© Macmillan/McGraw-Hill

At Home: Have your child write sentences with the contractions ***it's, we're, they're*** and ***you're.***

Name _____

- Remember that an apostrophe takes the place of the letter or letters that are left out of a contraction.
- Possessive pronouns, such as ***their, your,*** and ***its,*** do not have apostrophes.
- Do not confuse possessive pronouns with contractions. Some of them sound the same, but are spelled differently and have different meanings.

Possessive Pronoun	Contraction
their	they're
your	you're
its	it's

Read each sentence. Write the correct pronoun or contraction on the line.

1. (They're, Their) teacher is teaching a lesson about the moon. _____
2. (Their, They're) reading the book Rocket to the Moon. _____
3. (Its, It's) about the first lunar landing. _____
4. Are they almost finished with (they're their) book? _____
5. (Your, You're) reading a book called The Moon. _____
6. What is (your, you're) book about? _____
7. The book is about the moon and (it's, its) phases. _____
8. (Its, It's) full of interesting facts. _____

© Macmillan/McGraw-Hill

At Home: Have your child write each sentence above with the correct pronoun or contraction.

Name _____

- An apostrophe takes the place of the letters left out of a contraction.
- Possessive pronouns do not have apostrophes.
- The present-tense verb must agree with a pronoun in the subject part of a sentence.

Rewrite the paragraph correctly on the lines.

Were learning about the moon. Mr. Jones know a lot about the moon. Hes an expert! He say the moon cannot be seen at the start of it's cycle. Its called the New Moon.

_____

_____

_____

_____

_____

_____

_____

© Macmillan/McGraw-Hill

At Home: Have your child write about school, using present tense and contractions as possible.

Name _____

Underline two words in each sentence that could be used to form a contraction. Then write the contractions on the lines below.

1. The book I am reading is about a family in the future.
2. It is a science fiction story.
3. In the story, they are living in a new colony on the moon.
4. The dad is an explorer, and he is on a space mission.
5. The mom is a scientist, but she is also in a rock band.
6. It sounds like you are enjoying the book.
7. Someday we are going to live on the moon.
8. Do you think it is really possible?

1. _____ 2. _____

3. _____ 4. _____

5. _____ 6. _____

7. _____ 8. _____

© Macmillan/McGraw-Hill

At Home: Review this page together.

Name _____

- An **adjective** is a word that describes a noun.
- Some adjectives tell what kind.
  green balloons big balloons

Circle the adjective in each sentence. Underline the noun the adjective describes.

1. Luke is having a big party for his brother Paul.
2. He is making a chocolate cake.
3. He is putting vanilla frosting on top.
4. We are blowing up blue balloons.
5. I am hanging red streamers.
6. A funny clown will juggle at the party.
7. We got Paul a tricky puzzle for a present.
8. His parents got him new skates.

© Macmillan/McGraw-Hill

At Home: Have your child pick a favorite toy and use as many adjectives as possible to describe it.

Name _____

- An **adjective** is a word that describes a noun.
- Some adjectives tell how many.

Circle the adjectives that tell how many. Then rewrite each sentence using a new amount.

1. My birthday is in three weeks.

_____

2. I am inviting ten friends to my party.

_____

3. Mom is blowing up a few balloons.

_____

4. There will be nine candles on my cake.

_____

5. One candle is for good luck.

_____

6. There will be many sweet treats.

_____

© Macmillan/McGraw-Hill

At Home: Have your child write sentences that include adjectives that tell how many.

Name _____

- Use commas to separate three or more items in a series.
- Use ***and*** or ***or*** before the last word in a series.
  I see green, yellow, and pink balloons.

Find the mistakes. Write the corrected sentences on the lines.

1. Is Kenda's party on Friday Saturday or Sunday?

_____

_____

2. We will listen to rock disco and jazz music.

_____

3. Kenda will wear a red white or yellow dress.

_____

4. Her mom made cupcakes brownies and cookies.

_____

5. Kenda filled goody bags with whistles stickers and bubbles.

_____

_____

6. Kenda's aunts uncles and cousins are coming to her party.

_____

_____

© Macmillan/McGraw-Hill

At Home: Have your child write a sentence that lists three party favors. Remind him or her to use serial commas.

Name _____

- Use commas to separate three or more items in a series.
- An apostrophe takes the place of letters left out of a contraction.
- The present-tense verb must agree with a pronoun in the subject part of a sentence.

Find the mistakes. Rewrite the paragraph correctly on the lines.

Were throwing a surprise party for Maria Anna and Louisa. Their triplets! We'll serve sandwiches juice potato chips and chocolate cake. Were sure theyll be surprised.

_____

_____

_____

_____

_____

_____

_____

© Macmillan/McGraw-Hill

At Home: Have your child describe a party. Ask him or her to list the foods served using serial commas.

Name _____

Find the adjective and the noun it describes in each sentence. Write them on the lines.

1. Mom hangs colorful lanterns around the yard.

   adjective _____ noun _____

2. The full moon is shining in the sky.

   adjective _____ noun _____

3. We place the food on the four tables.

   adjective _____ noun _____

4. Yummy smells fill the air.

   adjective _____ noun _____

5. Three guests bring guitars.

   adjective _____ noun _____

6. They play some songs after we eat.

   adjective _____ noun _____

7. Grandma and Grandpa dance to their favorite tune.

   adjective _____ noun _____

8. Everyone says that it is a wonderful party.

   adjective _____ noun _____

© Macmillan/McGraw-Hill

At Home: Review this page together.

Name _____

- The words ***a*** and ***an*** are special adjectives called **articles**.
- Use the article ***a*** before a word that begins with a consonant sound.

  I read a book. I write a story.

Write the correct article *a* or *an* on the line to complete each sentence.

1. Our teacher told us _____ story.
2. It is _____ fantasy story.
3. It was about _____ dog named Leo.
4. Leo liked to chase _____ cat named Lola.
5. One day Lola got stuck in _____ tree
6. _____ firefighter tried to get Lola out.
7. Our teacher wants us to come up with _____ ending.
8. I'm going to write _____ happy ending.

© Macmillan/McGraw-Hill

At Home: Have your child make a list of objects at home that begin with a consonant and write ***a*** before each one.

Name _____

- The words ***a*** and ***an*** are special adjectives called articles.
- Use the article ***an*** before a word that begins with a vowel sound.

  I want to hear an animal tale.

Circle the correct article *a* or *an* to complete each sentence. Write the article on the line.

1. Have you heard the story about (a, an) ant named Azizi? _____
2. Azizi is (a, an) African name. _____
3. Azizi is (a, an) friendly ant. _____
4. He has (a, an) lot of friends. _____
5. One of Azizi's friends is (a, an) elephant. _____
6. He is also friendly with (a, an) kangaroo. _____
7. It is (a, an) interesting story. _____
8. What (a, an) great ending! _____

© Macmillan/McGraw-Hill

At Home: Have your child make up new sentences using articles ***a*** and ***an***.

Name _____

- Begin a proper noun with a capital letter.
- Begin an abbreviation of a person's title with a capital letter and end it with a period.

  Mrs. Ortiz read us a story.

Find mistakes in the sentences. Write the corrected sentences on the lines below.

1. mrs ortiz reads aloud a book by louis sachar.

_____

2. mr sachar won a newbery medal for the book holes.

_____

3. My favorite author is jon scieszka.

_____

4. I also like to read books by dr seuss.

_____

5. I hope mrs ortiz reads us a book by mr scieszka or dr seuss.

_____

_____

© Macmillan/McGraw-Hill

At Home: Have your child write a sentence using proper nouns and abbreviations. Check for correct capitalization and punctuation.

Name _____

- Use the article ***a*** before a word that begins with a consonant sound.
- Use the article ***an*** before a word that begins with a vowel sound.
- Remember to capitalize proper nouns.
- Capitalize a person's title. If it is an abbreviation, end it with a period.

Find the mistakes. Rewrite the paragraph correctly on the lines.

ms campbell read us a story about a old lady who swallows an fly. She also swallows an bird, an goat, and even an horse! I think the old lady should have gone to see dr doolittle. He's a animal doctor!

_____

_____

_____

_____

_____

_____

© Macmillan/McGraw-Hill

At Home: Have your child write a list of animals and then put the correct article ***a*** or ***an*** next to each animal's name.

Name _____

Write *a* or *an* to complete each sentence correctly.

1. I have _____ aunt who writes children's books.
2. She wrote _____ book called The Lion and the Mouse.
3. In the story the lion gets trapped in _____ rope net.
4. The lion lets out _____ angry howl.
5. _____ little mouse hears the lion's cry.
6. "I have _____ idea," the mouse says. "I will help you."
7. "How could _____ animal as small you help me?" the lion asks.
8. The mouse shows the lion _____ mouthful of sharp teeth.
9. Then it begins to chew on _____ piece of rope.
10. Soon the net has _____ enormous hole in it, and the lion is set free.

© Macmillan/McGraw-Hill

At Home: Review this page together.

Name _____

- You can use **adjectives to compare** people, places, or things.
- Add ***-er*** to an adjective to compare two nouns.
  Navy blue is darker than sky blue.

Underline the adjective that compares in each sentence. Write it on the line.

1. Orange is a warmer color than blue. _____
2. Green is a cooler color than red. _____
3. My painting is bigger than your painting. _____
4. Your painting is brighter than my painting. _____
5. Henry has a thicker paintbrush than Carlos. _____
6. Tess has thinner crayons than Jing. _____
7. Yael thinks painting is harder than drawing. _____
8. Art class is longer than music class. _____

© Macmillan/McGraw-Hill

At Home: Have your child compare two objects, saying which is longer, wider, heavier, and so on.

Name _____

- You can use **adjectives to compare** people, places, or things.
- Add ***-est*** to an adjective to compare more than two nouns.

  Cymbals are the loudest instruments of all.

Look at the pictures and read the sentence. Write an adjective that ends with *-est* on the line.

1. The harp is the _____ instrument.

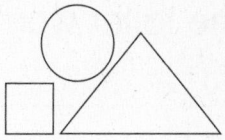

2. The square is the _____ shape.

3. Hannah is the _____ jumper.

4. Evan is the _____ runner.

5. Jenny is the _____ child.

© Macmillan/McGraw-Hill

At Home: Have your child draw three people or things and write a sentence using an adjective that ends in ***-est***.

Name _____

- Add an apostrophe and ***-s*** to make a singular noun possessive.
- Add an apostrophe to make most plural nouns possessive.

  Look at the one boy's painting.
  Look at the two boys' paintings.

Find the mistakes. Write sentences correctly on the lines.

1. The two artists paintings are colorful.

_____

2. The taller womans artwork shows a forest.

_____

3. The shorter painters artwork shows a garden.

_____

4. My three sisters favorite artwork is the garden painting.

_____

_____

5. My moms favorite artwork is the forest painting.

_____

_____

© Macmillan/McGraw-Hill

At Home: Have your child write a list of phrases that include possessives with the singular and plural forms of a noun.

Name _____

- Add ***-er*** to an adjective to compare two nouns.
- Add ***-est*** to an adjective to compare more than two nouns.
- Add an apostrophe and ***-s*** to make a singular noun possessive.
- Add an apostrophe to make most plural nouns possessive.

Underline the correct adjective to complete each sentence. Add an apostrophe to each possessive noun. Write the sentence correctly on the line.

1. Tims painting is the (bigger, biggest) of the five.

_____

2. Is Mayas painting (smaller, smallest) than Enricos painting?

_____

3. The three boys easels are the (neater, neatest) in the class.

_____

4. The second graders paintbrushes are (thicker, thickest) than the third graders brushes.

_____

_____

5. The teachers paintbrush is the (thinner, thinnest).

_____

© Macmillan/McGraw-Hill

At Home: Have your child write sentences with comparative adjectives and possessive nouns.

Name _____

Mark the adjective that completes each sentence correctly.

1. I had a _____ time than Irena had in pottery class.
   - O hardest
   - O harder

2. Maybe it's because she has _____ fingers than I have.
   - O longer
   - O long

3. The second pot I made was _____ than the first.
   - O nicest
   - O nicer

4. Irena made the _____ pot of all.
   - O prettiest
   - O pretty

5. She is the _____ potter in our class.
   - O finest
   - O fine

6. Of all the pots, Sam's has the _____ shape.
   - O odder
   - O oddest

7. His pot is _____ and more colorful than mine.
   - O big
   - O bigger

8. I painted my pot with the _____ red paint in the box.
   - O brightest
   - O brighter

© Macmillan/McGraw-Hill

At Home: Review this page together.

Name _____

- An **adverb** tells more about a verb.
- An adverb can tell how.
  The inventor worked slowly.

Circle the verb in each sentence. Then write the adverb on the line.

1. The scientist spoke clearly about her invention. _____
2. The audience listened carefully. _____
3. A volunteer pulled the lever gently. _____
4. The robot moved suddenly. _____
5. The crowd cheered loudly. _____
6. The robot bowed gracefully. _____

© Macmillan/McGraw-Hill

At Home: Have your child write a list of verbs and then write adverbs to go with them.

Name _____

- An **adverb** tells more about a verb.
- An adverb can tell when or where.
  An inventor visited our class yesterday. (when)
  She sat nearby. (where)

Circle the adverb in each sentence. On the lines, write the word *when* if it tells when. Write *where* if it tells where.

1. Long ago, George Washington Carver invented many uses for peanuts. _____
2. The peanuts grew outside. _____
3. Do you think Mr. Carver lived nearby? _____
4. Mr. Carver never sold his inventions. _____
5. Finally, Mr. Carver won a medal for his work. _____
6. Which of Mr. Carver's inventions do you use today?

   _____

© Macmillan/McGraw-Hill

At Home: Have your child brainstorm other adverbs that tell when and where and use them in sentences.

Name _____

- The pronoun *I* is always a capital letter.
- A proper noun begins with a capital letter.

  I visited an invention museum in Chicago.

Find the mistakes in capitalization.
Write sentences correctly.

1. i read a book about thomas edison.

_____

2. i learned that he had a laboratory in new jersey.

_____

_____

3. My dad and i are going to the edison museum in ohio.

_____

_____

4. i think edison's greatest invention was the movie projector.

_____

_____

5. One day i hope to be a great inventor like thomas edison.

_____

_____

© Macmillan/McGraw-Hill

At Home: Have your child write a sentence about their favorite invention. Have them use the pronoun *I*.

Name _____

- The pronoun *I* is always a capital letter.
- A proper noun begins with a capital letter.
- Add an apostrophe and *-s* to make a singular noun possessive.

Find the mistakes. Rewrite the paragraph correctly on the lines.

garrett morgan was an inventor from cleveland who worked to make peoples lives safer. morgans invention of the traffic signal made traveling safer. morgans' gas mask also kept people safe. i hope to create a life-saving invention one day.

_____

_____

_____

_____

_____

_____

_____

© Macmillan/McGraw-Hill

At Home: Have your child write a paragraph about an inventor he or she would most like to meet.

Name _____

Write the underlined word in each sentence that is an adverb.

1. Today, blood is kept in blood banks. _____
2. In the 1940s, Charles Drew discovered a better way to collect blood safely. _____
3. He also found a way to store blood longer. _____
4. People didn't know as much about blood then. _____
5. As a boy, Charles Drew lived happily with his family in Washington, D.C. _____
6. He got up early to sell papers on street corners. _____
7. His neighborhood had a pool nearby. _____
8. He soon became a star swimmer. _____
9. Charles Drew went away to college. _____
10. Later, he became a doctor and teacher. _____

© Macmillan/McGraw-Hill

At Home: Review this page together.

Name _____

- **Synonyms** are words that have the same or almost the same meanings.
- Use synonyms to make your writing more interesting.
  stones/rocks giant/big friend/pal

Choose the synonym from the box for each underlined word. Write it on the line.

like pals town wish mail hobby

1. Emily has a penpal named Tahira who lives in a <u>city</u> far away. _____
2. They <u>send</u> letters to each other every week. _____
3. Both girls <u>enjoy</u> writing. _____
4. Drawing is another favorite <u>activity</u>. _____
5. Emily and Tahira <u>hope</u> to meet each other one day. _____
6. They're sure they will be great <u>friends</u>. _____

© Macmillan/McGraw-Hill

At Home: Have your child list adjectives and then make up a synonym for each one.

Name _____

- **Antonyms** are words with opposite meanings.
- Understanding antonyms can help you better understand word meanings.

happy/sad loud/quiet large/small

Write an antonym for the underlined word. Choose a word from the box.

large slow mean tiny happy few

1. Our teacher read us a <u>sad</u> folk tale from China.

   _____

2. The tale is about a <u>huge</u> frog named Ling. _____
3. Ling was a <u>fast</u> hopper. _____
4. Ling had <u>many</u> friends. _____
5. One of Ling's friends was a <u>small</u> mouse. _____
6. She was a very <u>friendly</u> mouse. _____

© Macmillan/McGraw-Hill

At Home: Have your child list adjectives and then make up an antonym for each one.

Name _____

- Begin every sentence with a capital letter.
- End a statement or a command with a period.
- End a question with a question mark.
- End an exclamation with an exclamation mark.

Find the mistakes. Write sentences correctly on the lines.

1. what country are Abby's great grandparents from

_____

_____

2. they came all the way from Poland by boat

_____

_____

3. rahim's family is from Africa

_____

4. show me where Africa is on a map

_____

5. where is your family from

_____

© Macmillan/McGraw-Hill

At Home: Have your child identify each sentence above as a statement, command, question, or exclamation.

Name _____

- Begin every sentence with a capital letter.
- End statements and commands with a period.
- End a question with a question mark.
- End an exclamation with an exclamation mark.
- A proper noun begins with a capital letter.

Find the mistakes. Rewrite the paragraph correctly on the lines.

a new boy joined our class today his name is oren. do you know where Oren is from. he moved here all the way from Israel? "Please welcome Oren," said our teacher

_____

_____

_____

_____

_____

© Macmillan/McGraw-Hill

Name _____

Write *S* if the underlined words are synonyms.
Write *A* if the underlined words are antonyms.

1. The world is huge, yet sometimes it seems small. _____
2. Children in America are like kids everywhere. _____
3. We like to play, and we enjoy being with friends. _____
4. One sport that we all know is the game of soccer. _____
5. I like soccer because it's fast, but I like a slow game of baseball, too. _____
6. Do you think baseball is harder or easier than soccer? _____
7. My friend Sangeeta has always played soccer, but she has never played baseball. _____
8. My entire family was born in America, and her whole family was born in India. _____

Write a sentence. Use a synonym for *happy*.

9. _____

Write a sentence. Use an antonym for *noisy*.

10. _____

© Macmillan/McGraw-Hill

At Home: Review this page together.